My Diarrhe

Miranda Sings

GALLERY BOOKS

New York   London   Toronto   Sydney   New Delhi

Gallery Books
An Imprint of Simon & Schuster, Inc.
1230 Avenue of the Americas
New York, NY 10020

First Gallery Books paperback edition August 2019

GALLERY BOOKS and colophon are registered trademarks
of Simon & Schuster, Inc.

For information about special discounts for bulk purchases, please contact Simon & Schuster
Special Sales at 1-866-506-1949 or business@simonandschuster.com

The Simon & Schuster Speakers Bureau can bring authors to your
live event. For more information or to book an event contact the
Simon & Schuster Speakers Bureau at 1-866-248-3049 or visit our website
at www.simonspeakers.com.

Manufactured in the United States of America

3 5 7 9 10 8 6 4 2

Library of Congress Cataloging-in-Publication Data is available.

ISBN 978-1-5011-9216-6
ISBN 978-1-5011-9217-3 (pbk)
ISBN 978-1-5011-9218-0 (ebook)

Dear Diarrhe,

GUESS WHAT?!? I Found all my old diarrhe's from my Whole Entire Life when i was Looking for a snack underneeth my Bed. So i decided to tape them all together to make one huge **BOOK** that i can read whenever i want 2 rememBer all the memories i rememBer From my Memory that i can rememBer. So this is Basicaly my **AUTOBIOGRAFY**.

Too Bad their is so many secrets in it or else i culd sell it and make a ~~FORCHUN~~ FORTUNE! $$$

ANYways, my Foot is ichy so i shuld probly go. Bye.

Miranda

P.S. i Found 4 cheeseBalls under my Bed. SCORE!

i would Lick 2 dedicate this Book to **Myself.** cuz im the only person who is allowed 2 read it.

im serius. if you are reading this and you are NOT ME, STOP iT **RITE** **NOW!** i WILL make You regret it SO HARD. Thank you.

miranda
Jan 1, 2018
4:52 pm

TaBeL oF Contents

ABOUT THE AUTHER

Miranda Sings is

a incredibel singer, dancer, actor, model, magichan, etc. She alredy has a #1 ~~New York Times~~ New York Times Best selling Book, 2 seasons of her own Netflix original series, and many sold out world tours. She also has a cat. She is the most amazing, incredibel, Pefect, Beautiful, smart, talented genius in the world. she is also humble.

— miranda sings

Quotes from Celebrities—

"this is the best book I ever read."
- Miranda Sings

DO NOT READ! PRIVATE infourmashon

UNLESS ur name is Miranda Sings

and you look like this ➙

PUT. THE BOOK **DOWN**!...!,!,!

OK, now that its just me -

Hi Miranda. you look very grate today. enjoy your Book on you.

♡,

you.

Diarrhe #1

My Baby Book

OK, so i no this is tecknickly my BaBy Book and not a Diarrhe, Butt i was reading it and notised my mom got ALOT of stuf WRONG! so i had to fix it and now its a very educatchonal Book about me as a Baby. or as i like to call it → my AfterBirth. FYI- every time you see RED PEN marks, its me NOW Fixing my moms dumb mistakes so now, please enjoy, My AfterBirth.

My First Photograph

My Arrival

i wasnt waring any listick so i fixed it.

o.o.p.s. i spilled some brekfast.

wow! I was 114 pounds wen i was borned and now i'm 124. i only gained 10 pounds sinse birth! skinny legend.

Date of birth _Dec 24, 19__

Time of birth _9:34 AM_ ← This is A LIE! i never been awake that EARLY BeFORe.

Weight _11.4 pounds!_

Length _22 inches_ ← im at least 24 inches now.

Eye color _Black_ ← rasist.

Hair color _Brown_ ← no. it was DARK BROWN!!

Distinguishing characteristics _LOUD! Lots of hair._ relly pretty. Gunna Be FAMUS!

4

My First Footprint

Fixed it.

My First Bath

Clean and snuggly,
sweet and cuddly
yeh rite...!

see?
corn!

i LOVE sink baths! Mom always
washed me after doing dishes
so sometimes there was bonus
scraps of food floating in
the water!

My First Word

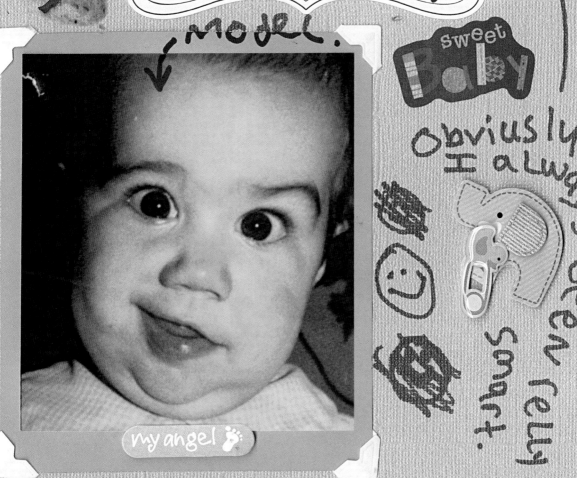

Miranda said her first word today. She pointed at me and said, "dumb." Now that is what she calls me. She's been doing it all day.

model.

sweet Baby

Obviusly I always been relly smart.

my angel

adorable

My First Haircut

This hare is Kinda yellow Butt mine is Brown so i colord it in to mach my real hare

my actual →
hare from 2day.
i wanred 2 compare it
with the baby hair. its a match!

My First Bed

Miranda refuses to sleep in her crib so she just sleeps on the floor whenever she pleases. I think she likes the Master Bedroom best so I'm currently moving out of it so she can have it. Having a baby is such an adventure! So fun. so neat. so... so... fun...

<<<

i cant Believe my mom Let People Walk on my Bed! Literly SO RUDE!

reLLY MOM? rakeen pics of me with no pants on? How am i supposed 2 sell my merch if im not waring my red swet-pants 24/7?

9

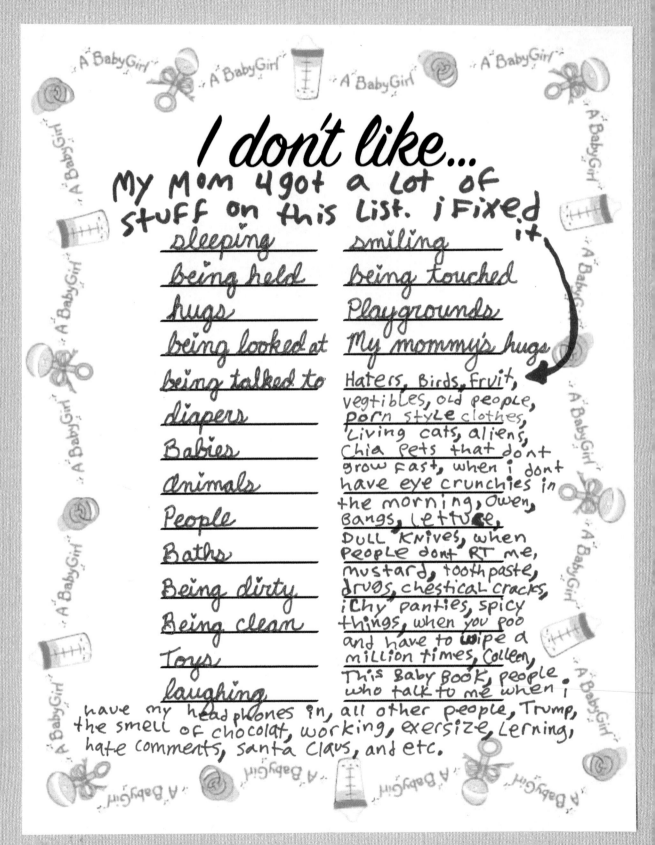

I don't like...

My mom 4got a lot of stuff on this List. i Fixed it

sleeping	smiling
being held	being touched
hugs	Playgrounds
being looked at	My mommy's hugs
being talked to	Haters, Birds, Fruit,
diapers	vegtibles, old people, porn style clothes,
Babies	Living cats, aliens, Chia pets that don't
Animals	grow fast, when i don't have eye crunchies in
People	the morning, Owen, Bangs, Lettuce,
Baths	Dull Knives, when people don't RT me,
Being dirty	mustard, toothpaste, drugs, chestical cracks,
Being clean	iChy panties, spicy things, when you poo
Toys	and have to wipe a million times, Colleen,
laughing	This Baby Book, people who talk to me when i

have my headphones in, all other people, Trump, the smell of chocolat, working, exersize, Lerning, hate comments, santa claus, and etc.

10

I like...

Eating.

_____   _____

_____   _____

_____   _____

_____   _____

_____   _____

_____   _____

_____   _____

_____   _____

_____   _____

_____   _____

_____   _____

Big News!

Miranda's going to be a BIG SISTER NO!

This never happened!!!!!

12

My Favorite Snack

Ive tried everything to get her to stop eating snails, but she loves them. I've heard rich people like them so I think it means she has very expensive taste. Isn't that neat?

she didnt menchon my Favy snaks NOW. i LICK meat and chees BALLS

ooh! i remember this one. it had Lots of BUBBLES wich made it extra squitshy and delitchus

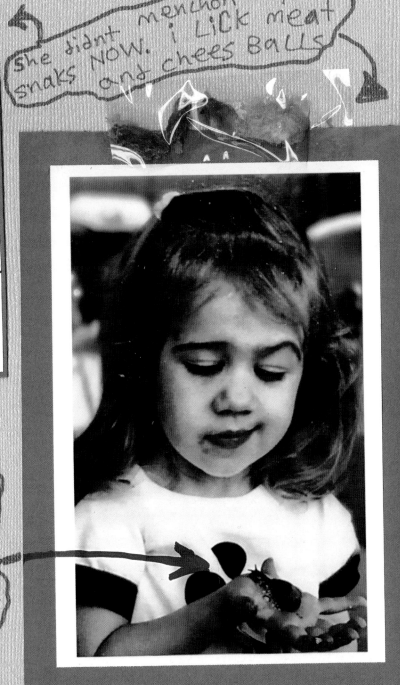

13

My First Friend

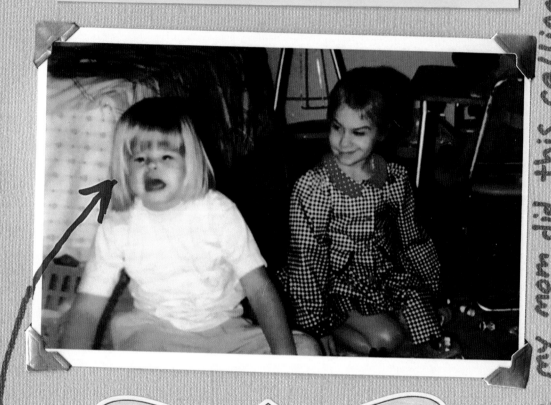

Miranda finally made a friend!
I paid the neighbor to let me
babysit her daughter for an hour.
She cried the entire time
and Miranda loved it! I love
seeing my baby girl smile.

OK, lets get 1 thing straight.
This girl was **NOT** my Frend. I
would NEVER be Frends w/ ANY1
who has BANGS Like that. Shes obviusly a murderer.

I cant Beleve my mom did this. calling yer 3 child
me a BABY wen im obviusly Like a 5 child??

My First Poo

she's here

splish splash

Thats a good one.

sweet baby

all wet!

cute

sweet

our bundle of joy

My First Pet

all Girl

i Fixed my Listick and hare.

THIS cat was SO RUDE! He ran away the day after i stole him from our nayBors house.

relly mom? Takeen pics of me with no pants AGAIN? i drew some on. Gotta sell that merch! www.mirandasings.com

This snake was dum. He wuldnt stay on my neck like a necklase so i set him free By Flushing him down the toilet.

i Finaly got a pet that i LOVED. He was my BFF. Charlie the fly. i dont no whos Bunny that is. i hate animols. gross.

My First ~~Sister~~

i don't have a sister

Miranda trying to break her ~~sister's~~ swing. Such a silly girl! ☺

This is the first time the girls touched. ~~Emily~~ started crying and then Miranda threw up. They haven't touched since...

Holiday Memories

The only holiday that matters is my Birthday and its Not on Here!!

Miranda did a four hour concert before letting the family open their gifts. She's so thoughtful.

4th Of July

Miranda wasn't happy about ~~her sister~~ getting a Christmas Present.

A fun Easter performance! Miranda is about to crucify herself. So cute.

19

Performing Memories

im Hungry.

Miranda has put on hundreds of plays and won countless TONY AWARDS (made by me of course.) Here are some of my favorite Performances...

Me and GOD wrote this play. i lived in that tomb 4 3 days. it was cold

BIBLE the Musical

Jesus Christ Superstar

WHAT? Those wern't REAL?!

Sound of Music

Les Miserables

Sweenie Todd

every single Performance was sold out. my mom was a gr8 audient.

Happy Memories

Miranda is happiest when she's eating ←TRUE.

(a big chunk of meat.....delitchus.

ew. who FoRce FeD me a vegtibl 21

Silly Memories

... its consequenses.

This is NOT silly its SERIUS! if you Boss me around their will be

I asked Miranda to pick up her toys and she ran outside and did this. She's so silly.

Miranda is always itching herself. My itchy little angel. Silly Girl!

This is Miranda's favorite T.V. program. I don't know what it is but it seems fun...and silly!

This is Terifying! I Cant Beleve I was wearing Pig tails! So Scary.

Miranda hugged me for the first time ever today. It made me cry. I will cherish that moment for the rest of my life. I love you, Miranda.

love You too Mom.

Diarrhe #2 is

my homeschool
work Book. in
this journal, i
discover my talents,
meet my Best
Frend, and Learn
Stuff.

Dear Bethany,

I regret to inform you that we can no longer have Miranda in our first grade classroom. She has continued to be quite problematic and I'm afraid we are not qualified to deal with a child with this many behavioral issues. We assumed you would discipline your daughter after we informed you that she "accidentally" flushed the class hamster down the toilet, and then urinated on the magic reading carpet for a week because she "didn't want the hamster to steal her pee."

It is obvious to us that you haven't dealt with this issue as we have noticed her behavior has gotten worse. She will not allow anyone to speak unless they are complimenting her, she is constantly singing and dancing on desks while I am trying to teach, and she locks children in the toy chest if they don't applaud for her all day long. Today she forced all of the students to lay on their stomachs on the playground to create a "stage" that she could tap dance on. Two students have broken fingers, one has a black eye, and Mrs. Srickland is still locked in the broom closet after Miranda superglued it shut so she wouldn't stop her performance. While we appreciate Miranda's confidence and bold personality, for the safety of our students and staff, we are no longer allowing her on school property. We strongly suggest you try homeschooling for a child with this many issues.

Sincerely,
Mrs. Zellet

OK, Mrs Zellet is a LIAR! Flushing that Hamster was NOT a accident!

My Sweet Miranda,

Welcome to your
new schoolbook!
I love you!
Love,
Mommy

i literaly have no idea wat this says. you have the worst hand writing in the world.

28

Deer Mom,

it is NOT FARE that UR makeen me do Homeskooling. im ONLY 8 years OLD and forsing me too do stuF is aBuse i think. im 2 busy 4 skool anyways. im trying to Brake the world record 4 how long someone can hold a little Bit oF dirt, and also my elbow is relly ichy today so i CANT DO SKOOL! DONT EVER TALK TO ME ~~again!~~ love Miranda

my dum sister ruined my pitchur!!!

P.S. can we have tater tots 4 dinner? 29

My Sweet Miranda,

I made a fun worksheet for you today! Please finish spelling the words by filling in the blanks.

I love you!

— Mommy

HI MOM.

2 ThiS iS

DUM!

Hahahahahahaha!

A+++

very creative! A++++++ I LOVE you! Love, mommy

My Sweet Miranda,

Today I think we need to work on something called "Manners". Please finish each sentence with something kind.   Love, Mommy

EXAMPLE:

May I please have a hug?

Now You Try! ♡

Please Stop talking.

Excuse me, You Smell Like a Fart.

Thank you for Literly Nothing

I'm sorry your So anoying

I love Me.   A+++   great effort, sweetie!

My Sweet Miranda,
Please practice writing your name
within the lines like this—
Miranda Miranda Miranda

Miranda Miranda
Miranda Miranda Miranda
This is IMPOSSIBLE!
Miranda Miranda
Miran miranda Miranda Mira
nda, The Lines,
Keep MOVING!
NOT FAIR!
I know it's difficult, Keep trying!
I love you!

32

good News mom! i
figurd out a easy
way to write in the
lines. just cover them up!

Miranda Miranda
miranda Miranda
Miranda. Miranda
Miranda
Miranda Miranda
Miranda Miranda Mirana
Miranda Miranda
Miranda

great work
sweetie! A+++!
A+++

33

Picture Day

Great job at your First homeschool picture day! Congrats on winning Most Photogenic in the whole school! I'm so proud of you sweetie!

A++++++! 💜 A+++

See? I told you home schooling would be fun! Love, Mommy

UNCLE JiM is a grate Photogafer. That dum doll was anoying tho. i want Fish stiks

okay sweetie!

34

My Sweet Miranda,

Today we are learning about ADJECTIVES.
An adjective is a word that describes
something.

 Example:
Miranda is beautiful!

Now you try!

Miranda is Me

Miranda is Me

Miranda is Me

Miranda is choking
a cat.

None of those words are adjectives, but you did
get all of the answers right. A+++++!

My Sweet Miranda,
Today I would really like you to try some math pretty please. I've made you a huge trophy for when you finish. I love you!

love, Mommy

$1 + 1 =$ __i__

$1 + 2 =$ __am__

$1 + 3 =$ __relly__

$1 + 4 =$ __hungry__

$1 + 5 =$ __BY.__

No oFense But i will Never need to No this. its Been proven you dont use math in Life

Mommy + Miranda = lots of love!

your a pervert.

you're right. I'm so sorry sweetie. I love you!

A++

36

Dear Mom,   Miranda Age 8, 2:01 PM
Please stop riting in
my skool book. Your
hand riting is so slopy
i can Barly reed it. its
so loopy. just tell me
my skool and ill do
it myself. also, How
cum my sister has a
~~diarekee~~ ~~diarree~~ ~~diary~~
diarrhe and i dont? NOT
FARE! So From now On
this is my skool Book AND
my diarrhe wich means its
PRIVAT! You cant read it!

OK, sweetie. I understand. I'm sorry! I love you! A+++

37

Deer Diarrhe— Miranda Age 8
Mom said i need 2
Pratice my cursive
on this page Butt
that is Boreen
and i just got relly
Busy cuz i got a
Posickle. i relly
wanted a Froze
toes Butt the Boy
outside only had a
rocket posickle. He
gived me it Free
Probly cuz he nos
Im Famus. That

38

Boy was relly werd
and had ugly shoos
and a Lout ike
Butt i hope he cums
Back tomorrow cuz
i dont Like oncy
seeing Mom and my
unkel every day.
Also i want another
posickle. That boy
is nise Butt also I
Like ise creem.
Love,
Miranda

Theres your cursiv MOM

my posickle stick

39

Dear Diarrhe, Miranda, Age 9 and 1/4 NUMBER 1

grate news! i Fired mom from Being my techer today. She was always telling me wat to do during homskooling so i was just Like "Mom stop talking or your Fired" so then she sayd "OK" and i was Like "YOUR FIRED" and then she cride. Butt now im my own techer. so im probly the First 9 years old techer in the world. im tired from riting this so i need to tack a nap OK By. miranda

Dear Diarrhe, Miranda
Age 9 and 1/3

My first day as a teacher went relly good. its very hard 2 Be a teacher AND a student so i made a skedule to Be organize

skedule

12:00 - wake up
12:30 - eat Brekfast
1:00 - rest
1:30 - eat Lunch
2:00 - rest
3:00 - teach miranda (me) skool work
3:10 - eat snak
3:30 - pick that scab
4:30 - rest
5:00 - eat snak
6:00 - eat dinner
7:00 - Homework (wach TV)
8:00 - eat a Lot
Later - go to Bed

Today in skool i teached myself a very important Lessen. How to cut the eyes out of my Barbys

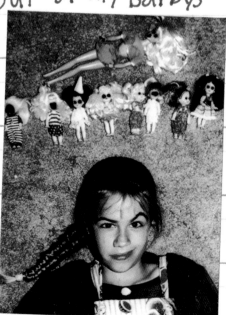

Dear Diarrhe, Miranda Age 9 and 1/9

i Found a ded Bird today. i took its Fethers to play with. it was Fun.

P.S.
i put the Bird Body under moms Bed to play with Later.

42

Dear diarrhe, Miranda Age 9½
Today For skooL i have
decided to teach my
self about My Favrite
snaks and Practice
eating them.

cheese BALL (crunchy!)

serial (soggy)

meat (squishy)

sprinkels (stale)

meat (cold)

Anyways, that
Boy with the
posickles cummed
over 2 my house

43

again today, i telled him
we can only hang out
if he dos everything
i say. He sayd "it wuld
Be my pleshur."
    hes wierd.
Anyways he has Been
Bringeen me posickles
For a lot of days
and a lot of peepol
are meen to him cuz
hes a loser no ofense.
Butt he Brings me

posickles and he is
Nice so i gived him
my stuff aminal sloth.
Hes my Best Frend.
Dont tell anyBody tho
cuz hes relly wierd.

also i ate
Fish stiks
For lunch
today. By.
Love,
MiRANDa

Hes holdeen
a posickle in
case i drop
the 1 im holdeen

Dear Diarrhe, miranda
age 10
6:01 pm
Today for skool i decided
to put on a HUGE Preformance
of CATS
at the Park! i Played
all the parts and
Uncle Jim Said i
was so good and im
gonna win a TONY! Butt
im not redy for a Boyfrend.
Anyways, after the
Show all the Boys were
so impressed
that they wouldnt
leave me alone.
These Boys
wanna Be with
me so Bad they
cant even keep
there shirts on!
wat a Fun day.
♡ miranda

me and my
cousins

Deer Diarrhe, ^{miranda}
Age who cares!

im haveen a HORIBLE
DAY!!!! First my Mom
told me 2 get out of
Bed wen i wasnt
even redy and then
my stupid Barby was
staring at me!! DONT
worry. i got her Back.
Butt im sick of Being
Disrespeted!!!

ANY eye crusties
this morning! TOTAL
RIPOFF! Not

P.S. i didnt even have

Love, miranda

47

Deer Diarrhe,
Today is a graTe
day! i decided im gonna
Drop out of home
Skool and Focus on
my modelling career!
Im so essited! My uncle
said the 1st step is to
make myseLF LOOK lick
a model. So he put lots
of pritty Lisstick on me
just like models do
and gave me a Fancy
Fur coat. i Look Amazeen!

48

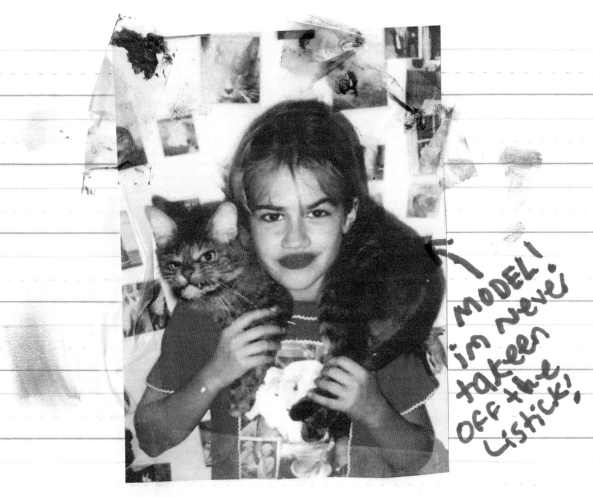

MODEL! im never taken off the listick!

So essited for this Netx chapter of my Life. im gonna Be FAMUS!

Diarrhe #3

Miranda's † PRAYER & JOURNAL

FOR GODS eyes ONLY!

Diarrhe #3 is my prayer journal from my pre pubescent years. I was around 11-14 years old when i wrote in this. Its a fun one cuz i talk to god alot, practise all my talents and becum a mime. However...... the end of this Diarrhe is relly scary. Beware.

Deer Diarrhe, Miranda age 11

Mom gave me this journal to rite my prayers in and "get out my emotions." i dont have any of those Butt it would be good to write to God so i can aks him to give me wat i want. so im sorry diarrhe, Butt im gunna caLL you God, or Jesus, or hevenly Father, or Daddy in this journal so i can get my prayers anseret easier. Ok, so. Hi God. PLease make mom give me that scooter.
Thanks.
in jesus name
gooDBYE,
miranda

P.S. Today i ate French fries and Lasania.

Praise the Lord in case you were wondering this is what i Look Like today.

Dear Jesus, miranda
Age 11

we need 2 talk. i took AMAZING
model shots at the department
store last week with uncle
jim and every day i look
for my pitchurs on the
cover of magizeens and its
STILL NOT THEIR!?!!
Not gunna Lie... im relly
frustrated with you God. i
have been praying that you
will make me famus for
WEEKS and it still hasnt
happened! i dont know why
your ignoring me so
tomorow im gonna go to
church and aks you in Person.
you cant hide From me 4ever...
     in Jesus name,   P.S. i had corn
        miranda   dogs 4 Lunch

        Praise the Lord

Hear are my model shots... so stunning.

im not a regular girl... im a cool girl.

i like how you can see my scalp here.

i call this pose "clenching it in."

me doing the splits

Praise the Lord

55

Dear Jesus,   Miranda
                Age 11
So as you no i went 2 church
today and mom FORSED ME
to go 2 Sunday Skool. Their was
a Bunch of girls waring
Pink WWJD Braslets and i
relly wanted 1 so i said
"Give me that Braslet! God sayd
You HAVE to or ELSE!" and
she didn't even do it!!!

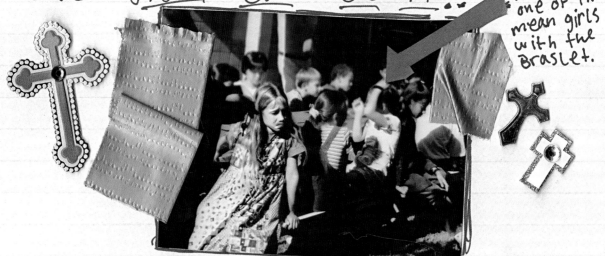

see? Thats
one of the
mean girls
with the
Braslet.

So you need 2 punish her. Thanks.
Anyways, then i realized if i was
Famus, i culd have all the WWJD
Braslets i want! So i started
Praying relly relly hard to
Becum more Famus right away
Praise the Lord

and suddenly, out of nowhere, a old man who smells like lettuce started passing out these flyers to everyone at church!!

THIS WEEK AT CHURCH

AUDITION FOR A HOLLYWOOD MOVIE!

Tonight - 6 PM - Casting Call!
Pastor Mike wrote a movie called "Drummer Boy!" and he is looking for kids to audition for the shepherd children. The movie will premiere on our local public access channel on Christmas Day.

Monday - Single's Night
Let Jesus introduce you to your future soulmate!

Wednesday - Youth group
Hey Teens! You know what's cooler than drugs? Our Heavenly Father! Come get addicted to your new best friend. Jesus is dope!

Friday - Mime class
Taking a vow of silence? BORING! Make it fun and become a mime! Preach the Word without saying a word!

Finally! you gave me the anser to my prayers and showed me a way to get relly Famos! im going to Becom a mime.

Thanks 4 ansering my prayers.
in Jesus name,
Praise the Lord miranda
P.S. Today i ate 3 cupcakes and a hot dog.

57

miranda
Age 12

Dear Heavenly Father,
that seems relly offichal.
can i just call you Daddy?
ill call you daddy.

Dear Daddy,
sorry we havnt talked in a
while, I Became a mime and
mimes arent aloud to talk.
at First i thought Being a
mime wuld help my modelling
career Becuz i thought it
stood 4 Models In Makeup Everywhere.

Praise the Lord

Butt it turns out Being a mime just means your trapped in a invisible Box a Lot. And I need to think **OUTSIDE** the Box. Plus those mime kids Were relly wierd. SO...
i Love you daddy Butt your idea to get me Famus through miming was <u>WAY OFF</u>. im Loosing my pashense, and im gonna ask you this one Last time. **God-PleaseMake me FAMUS!**
Rite NOW or else!
thank you.
Amen, Miranda

P.S. iF i dont wake up Famus i swear to God...
P.SS. i ate Mac and cheese with tuna and hot dog slices for dinner.

Praise the Lord

59

Dear Daddy,

miranda age 12

OK ＄ God, I have good news and Bad news. **BAD NEWS?** i woke up NOT famus. i asked you for ONE THING god. <u>**ON**E **LITTLE THING**</u>!

see? this is what a NOT Famus Person Looks like

i told Mom and Uncle Jim that you didnt make me Famus yet and Mom said, "Have fashense." Butt she knows Nothing. Uncle Jim was **SHOCKED**. He said you Blessed me with so many talents that you oBviusly WANT me 2 Be Famus so why hasnt it happend yet?! so hear is the **GOOD NEWS** ——— Uncle Jim is gonna Be my Manager! Now im for sure gonna get famus relly fast! SCORE! in Jesus name, Miranda.

AMEN

P.S. i wuld Like to pray for my hangnail. it relly hurts.

P.SS. Uncle Jim asked me to pray that his Lactos intolerens goes away cuz he had ice cream and he doesnt want diary-Ah.

P.SSS. i had *Praise the Lord* ice cream and fried chicken today.

60

Dear Jesus Daddy, miranda Age 12

Grate News! My ~~uncle~~ Manager is working relly hard to get me Famus. First order of Busness? Make a List of all my ~~talents~~ so my ~~uncle~~ Manager no's what hes working with...

My List of talents
- Singing
- dancing
- acting
- modeling
- eating
- talking
- Looking
- sleeping
- Picking
- itching
- drinking
- snacking
- Craft making
- whinning
- Being pretty
- Burning things
- T.V. watching
- staring
- teching
- Lerning
- jumping
- walking
- Living
- other

← He said he can work with this Butt my talents only count if the world sees them. so we snuck into my naybors house and i performed a original song i wrote called, "im Better then you." it was a hit! in Jesus Name,
me. miranda.

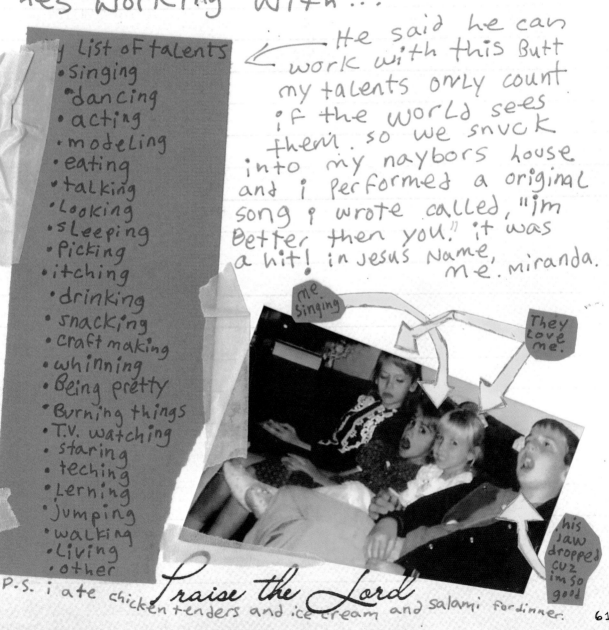

me singing

They love me.

his Jaw dropped cuz im so good

P.S. i ate chicken tenders and ice cream and salami for dinner.

Praise the Lord

61

Dear God,

Miranda
age 12

i have **a LOT** of prayer requests today. im having a <u>HORRIBOL</u> <u>DAY!</u> i went to church and i saw those girls with the **WWJD** braslets. i told them that im famus now and i have a manager and every-thing and they <u>**STILL**</u> wuldnt give me there WWJD braslets! **What the heck!!!** i even wore my fanciest pink dress that mom made me cuz it maches the braslet perfeckly!!! i thought ~~wwwwwwwwwwwwwwwww~~ ugh! my mom just came in my room <u>WITHOUT</u> <u>nocking</u> and then she left without closing the door behind her, wich im pretty sure is ilegal. See what i mean? horibol day. so here are my prayer requests...

• punish Courtney.
• give me her braslet.
• get me famus faster.
• make my mom stop being anoying.
• French Frys for Dinner.

♡ miranda AMEN.

This is wat the Braslet looks like → **WWJD**

Praise the Lord

62

Dear Daddy,

Miranda
Age 12

Thank you Lord for giving me a GRATE DAY today. i am so BLESSED. My ~~uncle~~ manager decided the next step to get me **RELLY FAMUS** wuld be to get epic new Headshots. wich is Grate Becuz i have a LOT of audishons cuming up. West Side Story, Grease, Wizard of OZ, Spice girls the musical, etc. my ~~uncle~~ manager said the only way ill get the lead in all those shows is if i have headshots that stand out and proove im better then any1 else. How do we do that?

ELEPHANTS.

elephants are the biggest, most epic, most famus animol in the world.

"You are the company you keep" - God. So if i have a elephant in my i think headshot, it prooves im the biggest, most epic, most famus person in the world. So we went to the zoo, and got the most incredibol HEADSHOT in the WORLD!

Praise the Lord

63

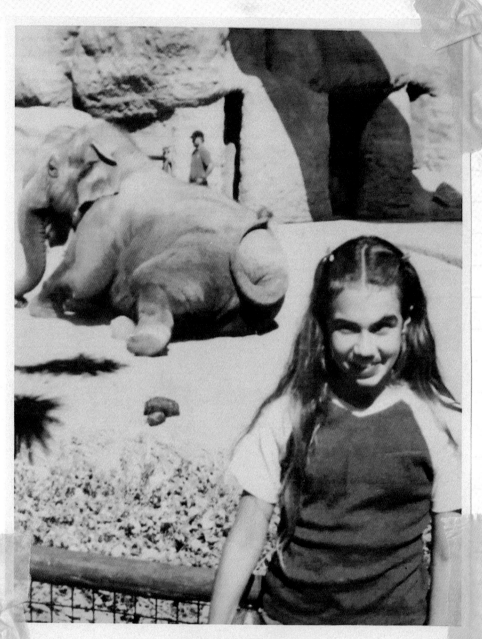

Miranda

see? incrediBol. i hope i get in all
the musicals! ♡ Miranda

Praise the Lord

P.S. Today i ate
pizza cuz im
trying to Be
healthier.

Dear God, Miranda Age 12

Grate News! The head
shot worked! i got the
lead in every single play!
Mom said they were the
Best homeskool plays we
have ever done in the Living
room! Thanks God. ♡ Miranda
Amen.
"Pray about it and youll get
Famus." - The Bible Probly

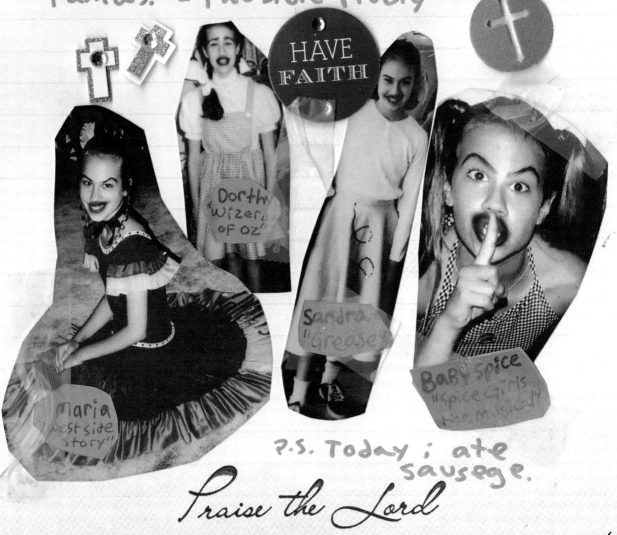

HAVE FAITH

Dorthi "Wizerd of Oz"

Sandra "Greose"

Baby Spice "Spice Girls the Musical"

maria West Side story"

P.S. Today i ate sausege.

Praise the Lord

65

Dear Jesus, Miranda
Age 13
i went to church today and did
this worksheet in sunday school

Faith

"For God so loved the world, that he gave his only Son, that whoever believes in him should not perish but have eternal life."
John 3:16

When was a time that you gave up something important for someone else?

One Time i gave up on school
For myself cuz it
was Boring.

"I can do all things through Christ who strengthens me"
Philippians 4:13

What does God give YOU the strength to do?

God gives me strength to rip my Barbys
heads off even when they are
on relly good. He also gives my ingrown
toenail strength to keep growing
Back.

"Love is patient, love is kind."
1 Corinthians 13:4

Who do you love enough to remain patient and kind for?

me.

66

its Been a while since i wrote to you cuz i have Been VERY Busy! Hear are all the things i have Been doing.

- My nayBor went on vacashon.
- i Lit a candel and took a Bath.
- i Burnt my hair on a candle.
- i stepped on a snail.
- i ate a Lot.
- i got a new Beanie Baby.
- i stepped on a very sharp crumb
- i ate aLot.

Butt i wanted to write to you cuz its Been MONTHS and im still not on the cover of ANY magazeens and im NOT super famus even tho ive aksed you a million times Butt i no im supposed to Be famus cuz look at me

So i think i no what the pRoBLem is, and i have figured out a soloshon. Your not redy to anser my prayers cuz im not taking my relashonship with you serius enough.

Praise the Lord so....

just married

We're getting married!

HusBands have to do whatever there wives want, so if we are married, you HAVE to make me FamuS. Girls at church are always saying "im dating Jesus!" well im marrying you. so stop dating those girls and make me Famus. also pay the BiLLs. love, Your, wife.

Praise the Lord

P.S. i ate a potato, grilled cheese, and chips today.

Dear Husband,

Miranda
Age 13

i have horribol News. i need to get a divorce. Mom said im Not allowed to get Married til im 21! Such a Rip off. So im sorry to Brake your heart, Butt i have no choice. Today has Been so Bad. i cant stop crying. Mom sayd she thinks im going thru PuBerty cuz im emochonal, irrashonal, and moody. Butt i dont no what shes talking about.

💔

me earlier today.

NOT LOVE,

miranda.

p.s. i ate ice cream, popcorn, and roast Beef casserole today.

Praise the Lord

69

Lord Forgive me 4 i have sinned.
i said a Bad word on accident. i hired
my BFF Patrick to Be my assistent.
Butt then realized theres a Bad
word in his job title. i was tricked
into saying it! Forgive me. it turns out
theres a Lot of words that trick
people to cuss, so i changed the names
to help people to stop sinning.

Assistent = Fannysistent

= Boobytanic

= Pooptzu
dog

= pooptakee
mushroom

= graBooty

= Tookie
cat

Let me no if their are other words
you need me to change 4 you God.
Forgive me. i Love u. Amen,
Miranda

P.S. i ate Bacon, Popsicles, Pickles, and Lunch
meat
today.

Praise the Lord

70

Dear Jesus,   age 13
i have a very importent prayer
today. i need you to punish my
mommy relly Bad. she
made me get Brases
and they hurt SO BAD!
This is child abuse FOR SURE!
I called the cops and they
didnt even arrest her. so
my prayer 2day
is that you
arrest her and
tech her a
Lesson 4 abusing
me! ALSO, i want
the prinsess diana
Beanie Baby. And
i want to Be Famus.
Love,
    Miranda AMEN
P.S. i ate tator tots
and cupcakes today. and
some chee Balls.
im smiling in Praise the Lord
this pic Butt dont be fooled. im
crying inside.

Brases are DUMB! I hate this!

71

Dear Jesus,   Age 13

Thank you 4 ansering my prayers. Mom slipped on a pile of my toys and broke her finger so she definitly lernd her lesson for giving me these braces. i also noticed shes getting a bald spot. You always go above and beyond to please me, Lord. That was a nice tuch. Thank you. My uncle took me to get model pics at sears, and im starteen to like my braces. Plus the rubber bands are fun to save. some times they have food still on them. im going to save them all. Thank you Lord. i am blessed. Love, mranda

AMEN

P.S. Today i ate 3 chees Burgers.

Praise the Lord

Dear Lord, miranda Age 13

Today at church the girls with the **WWJD Braslets** called me Brase Face. i am so exsited they gave me a cute Nick Name. i think it means im there frend now and they will give me a Braslet to mach theres! FINALLY!! i new you would anser my prayers! Butt mom is Being a <u>total</u> <u>Hater</u>. On the way home from church she said, "Those girls are not Your Frends.". Shes' so jelus of me!! i told her i need one of those Braslets Butt she just dosn't understand. its Not fare they all have 1 and i dont.

Whatever. Mom cant upset me today. My ~~uncle~~ Manager borrowd $500 from moms savings and got me fancy Profeshonal model pitchurs from a REAL Photografer! Hes gonna send them to all the magazeens to get me on a cover and get me FAMus! the pitchurs turned out

Praise the Lord Grate!→

73

see? they R so good.

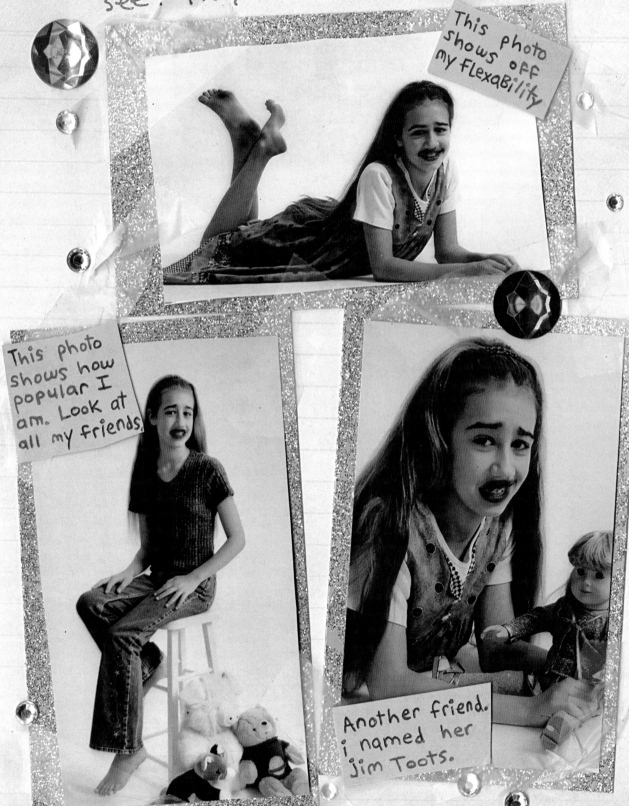

This photo shows off my FlexaBility

This photo shows how popular I am. Look at all my friends.

Another friend. i named her jim Toots.

This photo shows how much i hate plants

This photo shows off my sitting talent

This photo shows im a sofisticated model that always knows what time it is.

Amen, Miranda

P.S. i ate corn and ground beef today.

75

Dear Diarrhe, miranda
Age 13
4:27 pm
THIS IS THE BEST DAY EVER! Mom said
we are gonna go to a New church cuz
im 2 famus 4 the old one. Butt she
told me those girls gave her a
WWJD Braslet for me! **FINALLY!** They
told her that they love me and think
im too amazing 4 them. i agree.

Anyways,, it looks a lot diferent
From there Braslets Butt it maches
the dress Mom made me perfeckly!
Literaly the same materiel and
everything! im so Happy! Also my
~~UNCLE~~ manager sent my model shots
to all the movies and TV shows and
models so ill probly get super
Famus any day now. Nothing
can go wrong! MY LIFE is
PERFECT!

Praise the Lord miranda

P.S. today i ate tons of meat and also hot dogs.

76

GOD—
My period
started.
HOW COULD you do this to me?!
My LIFe is
OVER!
BYe.

Praise the Lord

77

Diarrhe#4 is

the journal i kept during my teenage years. its VERY emotchonal so Be prepared to cry. i had my First kiss, my First heartBrake, and my First viral video that changed ▮▮ my Life Forever...

♡ miranda

→ Dear Diarrhe, miranda age 13

My real tear drops!

This is the worst day of my Life! i almost Died. i was too upset before to tell you the story butt now i have this new jurnal and ive calmed down. Basicly my tummy was hurting and i that it was cuz i added too much kechup to moms cheesBall tuna casserole so i went to the Bathroom to get it out. all the sodden there was Blood in the potty! i started scree "I'VE BEEN SHOT!" my mom came in and said its just a period and she got hers when she was 13 too. SHE DID this to ME! SHE GAVE ME THIS DISEESE! i WILL NEVER FORGIVE HER FOR THIS! MY tummy hurts. MY diaper iches. im running away From home. BYE.

NOT LOVE,
miranda

81

Dear Diarrhe, Miranda
Age 14, 5:13PM

i've decided to put my career on hold. Obviusly i want to Be Famus Butt i just have 2 many emotchons rite now. i cant handle the stress oF Fame and try to deal with Becumming a woman. STOP pressuring ME!! i wrote some Poetry on My napkins at the taco place and i think they relly show my Feelings good.

Love, Miranda

Roses are Red
vilets are BLUE
i hate everyone.

Dear Everyone,
go away.
Love,
Miranda.

i never get anything i want
Their is Blood cumming from my Front.
i relly dont like anyone, that includes your son.
No one cares aBout me,
its annoying when i have 2 pee. (in the middle of the nite)
Life is totally UnFair
I Like steak medium rare.
my mommy is the dumBest
At Least i have BuBBle gum est.

82

Dear Diarrhe,

UGH! why do Bad things always happen to good people?! Today is AWFUL! im just trying to Be a good American sitizen and Live my Best Life, Butt so many Terrible things Keep happening to me that usually only happen in hell
PROBLY.

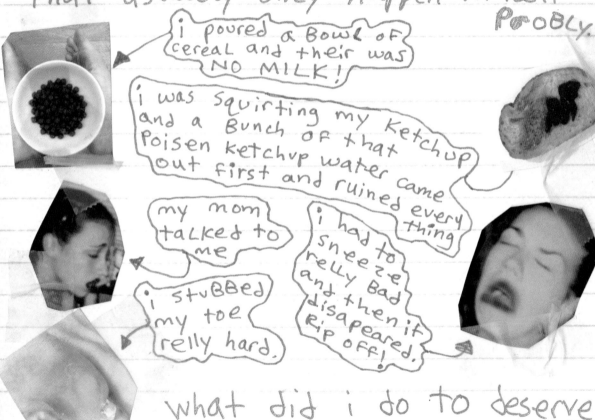

i poured a Bowl of cereal and their was NO MILK!

i was squirting my Ketchup and a Bunch of that Poisen ketchup water came out first and ruined everything

my mom talked to me

i had to sneeze relly Bad and then it disapeared. RIP OFF!

i stuBBed my toe relly hard.

what did i do to deserve all of these Satanic things? My Life is SO UNFARE! Anyways, gotta go! We are going to the movies and getting ice cream! Yay! Bye. ♡ Miranda

83

❤ ❤ Dear Diarrhe, ❤ Miranda ❤ Age 16

As you know, everything has Been totaly UNFAIR in my Life lately. My mom always wakes me up BEFORE my alarm, Barley any1 knows im famus still, every1 is annoying, and i hate everything. BUTT things are finally Looking up fOR ONCE iN MY LIFE! i have huge News! Are you redy for it? i have... A BOYFREND! My First Boyfrend! can you Beleve it?!? Hes relly cute and His name is Michael! we have Ben going to the same church for a while Butt this sunday he made it offishaL! HE SAT NEXT TO ME AND HELD MY HAND! Your only suposed to do that with your wife so. Things are moving relly Fast. And honestly i think he would have done it even if the paster didnt say "Lets all hold hands for prayer." He pulled his hand

84

away half way thru the prayer and his hand was pretty limp butt i think he was trying to be respecful since we arnt married yet. Also my hand was pretty wet so he probly relly loved that and didnt want 2 lust over me. oh! and get this! he's also my SUGAR DADDY! He gave me $#$! They passed around a ~~____~~ donate plate at church and he put 5 dollers in it, handed me the plate and SMILED! im not Dum, i no what that means. So i took the 5$# and winked at him relly hard. Then he moved seats.
I HAVE A BOY FREND! i cant wait til church on Sun day so i can see him again! i LOVE him!

Miranda and Michael

Miranda

kissing

michael

★ **Dear Diarrhe,** Miranda Age 16

my relashonship with Michael is going relly good. Every day this week i went to his house when he was at school to get to know him Better. i've learned that he likes the spice girls, cheetos, and the organ trail. i got on his computer yesterday and tried to win it 4 him as a suprise Butt i acsidentally died of dysentary.

He must know im cumming every day cuz he leaves the window unloked for me. He's so thotful. i gave him this letter ————————⟶ at church on sunday and he opened it and then gave it Back and walked away. i literaly left him speechless! i LOVE him so much! i cant wait till we are married!

♡ miranda

2 my ♥ BOYFREND michael ♥

♥ Thanks 4 makeen our relashonship offishal By Holding my Hand at church Last week. Sorry i killed you of Dysentary. i hope your not mad. if you are thats relly imature cuz i was just trying 2 help so u Better stop Being mad RITE NOW. is this our First Fight?!? Your Being a JERK. im sorry. i hate wen we Fight. i love you.

ANYWAYS, i just wanted to say even tho im hotter and more Famus then you, i think this can work, even tho i'm WAY out of your Leeg. Your SO LUCKY. Do you Like this cat? i took him from my neighBors Back yard and every nite i put flowers on him in Bed and pretend its you. Butt dont worry! Tonite i'll come to your house and do it to you insted of the cat. i cant wait! i LOVE YOU! cant wait 2 spend the rest of my life with you! Love you.

♥ Miranda

PS. if i ever see you with another girl your dead meat.

87

Dear Diarrhe,

ok, so Michael is playing hard to get and its relly annoying. i get that this is just his way of Flirting Butt its gonna Be hard for our relashonship to grow if he keeps running away from me, and locking his doors and windows so i cant get in his house. At church the other day i gave him a Bag of relly thotFull presents and he handed it Back and ran away. Hes so sweet. He new how much i wuld love all the stuff in the Bag so he wanted me 2 have it.

Miranda

P.S. valentimes day is cumming up and he Better propose!

Candy.

a Lock of my hair for romance.

a delichos chicken nugget

my favorite vegtible.

my Bandaid

88

Dear Diarrhe, ^{Miranda Sings}
7:42 pm

i am HartBroken!!!! i had 2 💔
Brake up with Michael today. i
went to his house today and he was
packing things into a truck. This is the
hartBraking conversashon we had —

Michael—"i can see you in the Bushes.
please stop."

Me —"where are you going?"

Michael—"im moving"

Me—"your Leaving me???"

Michael—"Yes. We are moving 2 Utah"

Me—"i cant Beleve your Braking up with me+"

Michael— "im Not Your BoyFrend!"

Me—"i know! Cuz we just Broke up you
jerk! You dont have 2 rub it in!
Fine! im Braking up with YOU!!
its over!"

Hes Being a Total Brat But i no
he Loves me. Valentimes day is
next week so im sure he will
apologize and we will Live hapilly
ever after. i Love him so much.

♡♡ ♡ ♡ miranda ♡ ♡ ♡

89

Dear Dum Diarrhe, Miranda Age WHO CARES

Valentimes Day is SO DUM! People who arnt in a relashonship are reminded all day that they R alone 4EVER and people who DO have a relashonship stress about makeen the day perfekt. its a loose loose situashon!!!!! i dont even care that im single on Valentimes day. Stop saying that i care cuz i DONT! i dont care that Michael wont call me back. i dont care that he didnt give me a valentime or say thank you 4 the one i gave him. i DONT CARE! im going to be alone forever and i DONT CARE! The only reason i got mad today is cuz i took a bite out of one of the chocolates mom gave me and it had a freaking cherry in it! i might as well eat POISEN cuz its the same thing! fruit has NO PLACE near chocolate! Valentimes Day is RUINED! i will NEVER selebrate this holiday! I HATE IT!!!!
(unless Michael asks me out. that wuld be so cuuute! ♡♡)

NOT LOVE,
Miranda

91

Dear Diarrhe,

my dum mom is FORSING ME to do chores. This is child ABUSE! Well jokes on her cuz when i was dusting i Found dust. $Cha Ching!$ im gonna Be a million nair. im gonna make my own Line of dust stuffed aminals, sell them, get RICH and move out! Then mom will miss me so much and regret Forsing me to do chores. Best revenge ever!

$ $ $ $

Buhddust
$200.⁰⁰

Dirt Dessert
$150.⁵⁰

Lintley Spears
$540.⁴⁹

Albert Grimestein
50¢

Hairy Potter
$1000.⁹⁹

im gonna make a Forchune!
♡ Miranda

92

Dear Diarrhe,

oh my gosh!! Today i had my **First Kiss** Finally! it was so amazing and super fun! i was relly nervus cuz i had never done it Before Butt it was Better than i culd have imagined. **AND** — it was a French Kiss! can you Beleve it? OK, so hear is the story—

OBviusly things didnt work out with Michael Butt i knew i was redy 4 my first kiss anyway. So... i sat down on my Bed, and kissed My Knee. i did it for Like 5 minutes it was relly romantic and tasted like cheese Balls wich was a Big Bonus. i am on cloud 9! im in LOVE!

Miranda

93

Dear Diarrhe, miranda

sorry i havent written in hear in so Long! **its Been Years!** Butt i've **BEEN BUSY GET OFF MY BACK!!!** Lets see...what have i Been up too... i got a pink Jacket, i Found a new Brand of hot dog i relly like and my career is aBout to exPLode. Uncle Jim got a video camera so we can upLode viteos of me to the interntet and show the world my talents. i guess their is a WeBsite caLled **YouTuBe** that he wants 2 use. We are gonna FiLm the First one today. Oh! ALso — i have a relly good sCaB Forming. Gotta go. Uncle Jim wants to Film this video. ♡

miranda

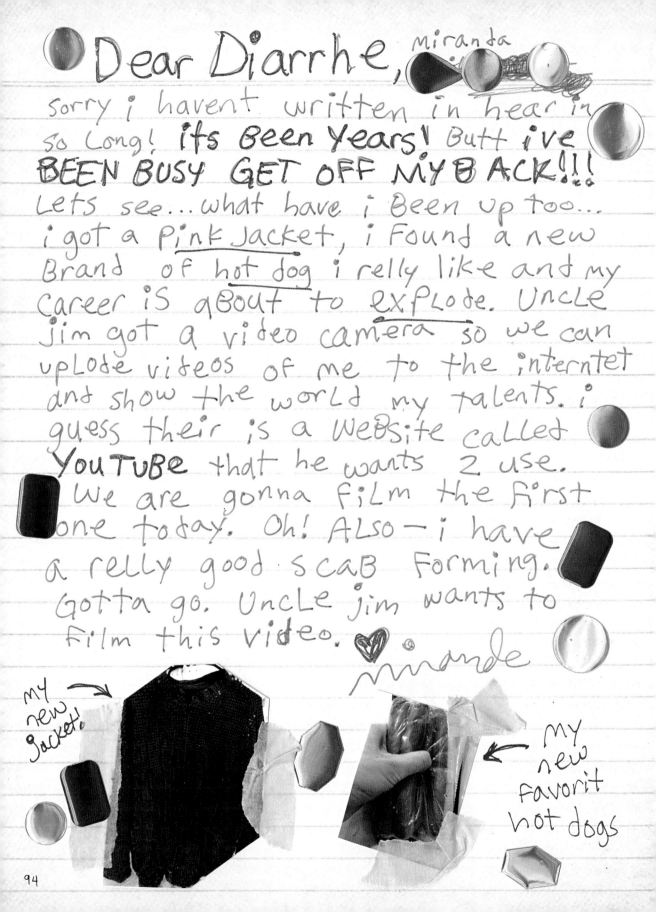

my new Jacket!

my new Favorit hot dogs

94

Dear Diarrhe,

a **LOT** has happened. We uploded that video and it got a **TON** of views, Like 49! My uncle came up with this 5 phase plan to get me Famus. We are hafway thru the Fazes so i shuld be Famus pretty soon. i did a big preformence in the big Attle (seattle) and my uncle let me borrow his **red swetpants.** They feel good in all the creeses so im gunna start waring them all the time. THEN we did **ANNIE** in the back yard. Butt it got ruined cuz some1 clogged the toilet. Patrick played Daddy WarBux and i played annie and something weird happened. i felt relly gassy and floaty when we did the romantic scene. Anyways i gotta go becum a magichan.

miranda

p.s. im the one who clogged the toilet.

95

Dear Diarrhe,

uncle jim is relly anoying me. his dumb 5 faze plan to get me famus is taking **For EVER** so im just gonna get myself famus on my own. i dont no how yet Butt ill figure it out. i shuld Be the **most** Famus person in the **world** By now! **ugh!** Being me is relly hard. **and** to make matters **worser**, Uncle jim keeps talking aBout uploding a video that i **DONT** want him 2 post. its called "Free Voice Lesson" and it gives away **aLL** my singing secrets! hes such a idiot.

Anyways, i didnt poop yet today so at lesf i have that to look forward to. gotta go. Full house is on. BY. ♡ miranda

96

Dear Diarrhe,

Uncle Jim uploaded that video.
it went viral.

Free Voice Lesson
MirandaSings08 6 Videos

102,684

601 likes 489 dislikes

Diarrhe#5

2009   2009

Private! only uncle Jim can read!

Diarrhe #5

is the journal i kept
rite after i got my
first viral video. i
was roBBed, cheated,
and Disrespeted. Butt
i never stopped
Begging people to
give me money and
make me Famuser.
#NeverGiveUp
#ImAnInspirashon

Dear Diarrhe,

a **LOT** has happened since i last wrote to you so i decided to get a new diarrhe. Hear is every thing that happened since we last talked:

- i got famus
- i got a BoyFrend
- my whole family and BF Left me.
- i got them Back
- i ate a LOT of CheeseBalls
- went to NYC with my Dad.
- i got MORE Famuser
- my dad left. hes dumb.
- i came home to my Family
- i ate a popsicle
- a girl named Colen is impostering Me.
- we got evicted.
- i got a hangnail.

So thats what you missed. im Literaly so stressed. And to make matters worse, i stepped in a tiny Puddle in the Bathroom in my **SOCKS**! Now i have a soggy toe. BYE! ♡, miranda

⭐ Dear Diarrhe, 🔘 miranda sings
may 3, 2009, 3:29pm

So uncle jim and me desided to go on a **WORLd tour!** We want to do it for 3 reasons —

① cuz im famus
② to find my imposter Colline
③ Frankie Grande (a guy i met in NYC) said i can always call him if i need anything at all.

So we are gonna tour to NYC, get me on Brodway, and make Frankie give me his apartment.

By the way, this is my imposter ➜

im way prettier then her.

her eyebrows look like somthing i lerned about in health class

i can see her chesticak crack! porn!

Frankie and me last time i was in NYC. i gave him a voice lesson.

Uncle jim said we dont have any shows booked for this tour yet butt hes pretty sure if we just show up at venues they will let me preform. Hes such a good manager. ok time to go to our first show!

♡ miranda sings

102

⭐ **Dear Diarrhe,** miranda Sings
May 4, 2009 5:21PM

im writing to you from inside the Mini van on TOUR! We are in PortLand now wich im pretty sure is a different cuntry. ALL the people hear seem foreign. They all have Big mustashes, lots of tattoos, they only eat coffee, and they all want to Be Farmers. im having culture shock Butt LuckiLy im ⅛ PoLish so i understand the Language Pretty good.

We tried to get on stage during a comunity theater preformance OF OKLAHOMA Butt we got Kicked out. We also got Kicked out of a "LiBerals only coffee shop," a "animal free Circus," and 5 farmers markets for trying to perform. TOUR Life is so Fun! ive Been uploading to YouTube aLoT lately! Hear are sum of my faurites-

"my fist Music video Genie in a BottLe"

"SingLe Ladies"

"im relly sick. spoon full of sugar"

"respect"

We just got to Our next stop! WISh me LUCK! ♡ miranda ⭐

Dear Diarrhe, Miranda Sings May 2009 :59 PM

Tour is going grate! We just finished our first show! This is a pitchur of the audience we had!

Those Ladies mite Look quiet Butt they were rowDy! in the middle of my opening number one of them yelled "BINGO!". She oBviusly got my name wrong Butt i Forgave her after i kicked her out. Well, im exhausted and i have to ~~pee~~. Tour Life is crazy! Good Nite. Love, Miranda

Dear Diarrhe,

Today i did a show in UTAH! Normaly we just show up at theaters and hope they Let us in Butt this time a guy called and said he wuld give me my **very own show** at the kids museum he works at! We snuck in after it closed. i asked if it was Legal and he said he turned off all the security alarms & cameras. i got to decide wich kid area to perform in. i almost chose the kid size grosery store Butt i ended up picking the kid size oval office cuz im probly gonna Be precident soon. We sold 40 tickets at 30 dollers a pop! i dont no how much that adds up to cuz im not a scientist Butt my uncle says it over $1,000 so that means **we are gonna Be MILLIONAIRS!** ♡, Miranda

me performing in my oval office

the audiense got to sit on kid chairs.

Dear Diarrhe,

UGH! that guy from Utah **STOLE OUR MONEY!** when we called him to get paid he said hes gonna keep all the money cuz he used a lot of gas driving to the museum 4 my show. i kinda understand cuz i herd gas is espensive Butt he shuld at lest give me a cupple <u>dollers!</u> Then he **Blocked** our phone # so we culdn't contact him anymore. **Ugh!** Uncle jim says this is a good thing cuz now i have a scandal and when the news picks up the story ill get even more Famuser.

   ANYWAYS, we found a pretty chair in someones yard 2day and did a photo shoot with it. im gonna send a copy to santa to prove ive been a good girl.

im also gonna send a copy to that guy in Utah to tech him a lesson. Bye.
miranda

i've Been a very **VERY** good girl... xoxo

For santa

For dumB utah guy

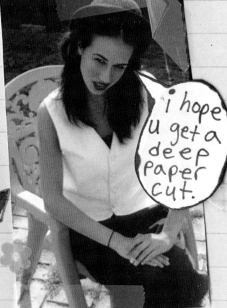

i hope u get a deep Paper cut.

❀Hi Diarrhea,

miranda sings
may? 2009 11:12 am

we drove around for a **LONG TIME** today
Looking For New York City. We dindt
Find it Butt we ended up in **Sacamento, CA!**
i thot Sacamentos were just those red
things inside green olives, ⟲→ sacamento.
Butt it turns out its a city too. ●
We found a choir concert at a school
so i went on stage and decided they
wuld Be my Backup singers. The
choir conducter waches my videos so
he didnt call the cops! it was my
Best Preformance on tour so far!

Bohemien Rapsidy

YMCA

The choir techer even let us sleep at
his house witch was nice cuz im
sick of sleeping in the car. Hopfully
we will make it to NYC soon, cuz
this tour is getting relly hard.
gotta go. i just found a ingrown hair
and i relly wanna get it. BYe.
♡ miranda

107

🌸 # Dear Diarrhe,

im not sure where we are Butt i think its the middle of nowhere. So mayBe Lompoc? Uncle jim rented out a theater For my show 2nite! it costed all the money we have Left Butt he is confident we will make the money Back in ticket sales. So we are gonna go 2 the sizzler to pass out these fliers to promote the show. ➡

Every1 loves Sizzler so i Bet my show will Be Sold out! THINGS R LOOKING UP! NYC HEAR WE CUM! ♡

Miranda

SO YOU LIKE BUFFETS HUH? THEN YOU'LL LOVE THE FAMus **MIRANDA SINGS** FROM YOUTUBE!

PERFORMANCE TONIGHT!
ONE NIGHT ONLY!
the high school down the street. $5 per ticket

Dear Diarrhe,

The show just ended. Only 10 old Ladies showed up. Butt i was doing the Best Performence of my Life so i dindt even care. The Feeling i felt on stage was so amazing. it Felt Better then the Feeling of a Q-tip deep in your ear after a shower. Better then when you pick off a scaB in one peace and it doesnt even Bleed. Better then every Mary kate & Ashly olsen movie comBined. Butt then..... something terriBLe happened. Every1 started walking out of the theater. What the heck! im Famus. How could this happen to me?! Old Ladies who can Barely walk... WALKED OUT OF MY SHOW in the Middle OF THE PREFORMENCE! well... tecknicly one rolled out in a wheelchair. and a couple of them scooted out on walkers...Butt still!!! HATER! They will regret it. just wait and see. im gunna proove those old Ladies wrong. WOAH! a Big Bug just hit the windsheeld. That was proBLy God telling me im gonna get revenge on those Ladies. Thanks Big guy. You always got my Back. ♡

Miranda

109

Dear Diarrhe, Miranda Sings May 2009

i have Bad news and good News.

BAD NEWS= Uncle jim said we are Broke so we have 2 put tour on Hold.

GOOD NEWS= i started a new Busness so i can get rich and keep touring. We are in california and what do all Californians Love? **Beaches.** So im gonna sell **SAND!** i got the idea when i took off my Bathing suit after a Long day at the Beach and found clumps of sand in their. i cant just waste it and throw it away! Plus this sand has tuched me so its probly worth a Lot of money. im gunna Be a Millionair!

this one hurt in the crevises

♡ Miranda

Venus Beach $200.00

This one was so soft in my skin

MaLiBoo Beach $50.00

This one hurt in my Bathing suit

Newporn Beach $4.99

goLeta Slough. $34

This is my favurite. it was in all the plases

110

Dear Diarrhe,

Miranda Sings
May 2009 6:22 PM

You will NEVER BELEVE all the stuff that happened 2day! First - a Big Producer said he wanted me to Be in "Guys & Dolls" on Broadway! so i met him in L.A. and he said i was casted! Butt then he said "Before rehersals, i want you to do a video with me and Let ME Be the one to reveel your true identity to the world! your real name is coalleen, rite?"

~~YGatt ucy PXoA At~~

i told him he can NOT do that and then he said i wasnt in the show anymore! What the heck! That dumB imposter is ruining my Life! THEN i got a call from a theater in Miami, Florida that wants to Book me! Butt i dont have money for a plane ticket so i dont know how im gonna get their. Good News is, i think Miami is next to NYC, so if i can get their i'll Be golden. ♡ Miranda

P.S. my sand Busness didnt work out. i only sold 1 Bag of sand.
P.S.S. my knee is VERY ichy today.

111

Hi Diarrhe, Miranda Sings
May 2009 2:19 PM

i made it 2 **Miami**! it turns out the guy who Bought a Bag of sand From me is a **Big Fan** of my videos! His name is Ryan, and he asked me 2 sing at his Birthday Party at a gay CLUB in LA. and **GUESS WAT?!** He paide me! 200 dollers! it only paid for 1 flight to miami so i took it and Uncle Jim stayed in California with my grandma. The show is **TONITE!** And then ill Be rich and Famus, go to NYC, tell Broadway to give me a show, make Frankie give me his apartment, Find my imposter and tell her to **BACK OFF**, and Live hapilly ever after. im so essited!

♡Miranda

me preforming at Ryans B Day Party →

THings are Finally working out!

112

Dear Diarrhe

THings are NOT working OUT!!!
while i was performing on stage
everything in my dressing room got
stolen! i didnt panick too much cuz i
knew i was aBout to make a lot of
money from my show. Butt the theater
manager said she didnt need to
pay me cuz we didnt have a contract.
SO UNFAIR! i cant help that God
made me perfect with 20/20 vishon
so i dont need **glasses** or **contracts!**
ripoff... **im SICK of THIS!** Ive Been on
tour for ~~months~~ ~~weeks~~ days and ive
delt with people rejecting me, ive
Been sleeping in a car, i havent
had <u>any</u> supersize fries - only regular,
and now ive Been roBBed. **i thot**
Famus people were supposed to have it
easy and get everything they want!
So i did what any sane person would do
in my posishon. i called my rich, famus
frend and Begged him to give me money.
After all, Frankie <u>DID</u> say "call me if you
need anything at all!"... i definitly need
anything at all rite now. i hope he
calls me Back soon cuz i relly need to
pee. ♡ miranda

113

⭐ Dear Diarrhe,

Miranda Sings

EVERYTHING worked out! iM Famus! i KNEW i was Famus! i KNEW i wuLd proove those old Ladies wrong! idiots... SO... Frankie Grande ended up Flying me to NYC and he let me stay with him. He wuLdnt give me his apartment wich i think is relly rude, Butt im thinking aBout changing the Locks next time hes not home.

ANYWAYS, ALOT has happened in the Last couple weeks! iLL try to summ it up in the next couple of pages. ♡ Miranda

i performed with Frankie Grande aLot in NYC. i think we R dating. i got relly close to his mom and sister while i was there too. im gonna start giving his sister Ariana voice Lessons. she relly needs my heLp.

i performed with the
Brodway cast of Mama
Mia at a Big Event.
Someone Filmed the
hole thing so if i ever
wanna wach it again i
can just scan this code.
(P.S. i Blurred the faces
of the people idht like)

video of
me and Mama mia

video of
me at
Brodway
on Brodway

This is seth
rudetskey. i
never herd of
him Butt hes
Famus and i met
him when i snuck
on stage at
Brodway on
Brodway in
Time square

115

LONDON.

i went to LONDON! A produser said he could get me on stage in the west End. i didnt wanna go cuz "the west end" sounded like a gang and i dont like guns. Butt then he said the west end is like Brodway butt for people with British accents. so i went and suddenly my experiense in the West end went SOUTH. Somehow i ended up on stage with the cast of "Naked Boys Singing". it was TRAMOTIZING! i spent the hole show trying to cover up their privases.

if anyone ever saw this it wuld RUIN my career.

116

Hopefully those are the Last naked Boys i will ever see. The rest of my trip to London was grate! i performed with TONS of People from the west end. (the singing and dancing kind. Not the gang kind.) so other then the naked nightmare, i Loved London. Somehow i understood every one Perfectly even though i dont speak British! i guess im just relly smart. ♡, Miranda

Some videos of my West End Preformenses.

me Preforming at a school dance or something

taking pics with Fans at a gay Bar.

me and the west end cast of Chicago

IRANDA TEACHES ROCK OF AGES

i Flew Back to NYC after London and Preformed a Lot more! i gave the Brodway cast of "rock of ages" a voice lesson cuz they needed it relly Bad. Hears the video from it.

i performed at jim Caruso's cast Party. Jim said i can do my own 1 women show at Birdland Jazz cluB whenever i want. He said im gonna Be a STAR! oh and this is some anoying girl i Performed with.

And last Butt not Least, i Found that dum imposter, coalleen. She said shes not gonna stop impostering me cuz it gets her views. She's so obsessed with me! so we decided to make a deal. i cant tell you what it is cuz its TOP SECRET and i wuld have to kill you, Butt we made a video together. im pretty sure i dont have to worry about her cuz shes kinda ugly and not talented (no offense) so she will never get Famus. its proBLy the Last time i will ever hear about her to Be honest.

This is the video we did together. SHe is not good.

ANYWAYS, im Back home in Tacoma now. its Been a crazy month, Butt im so glad everyone Finally knows im Famus. From now on, ill Be Living a classy, Fancy Life FULL of GLitz and GLamer!!! Gotta go... uncle jim is clipping his toe nails and i like to watch.
♡ miranda

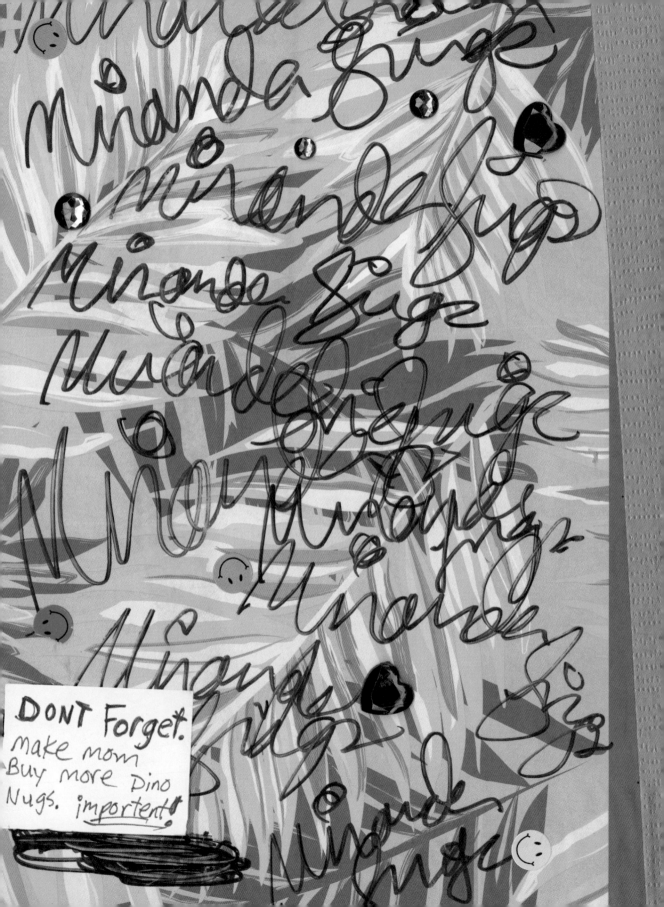

DONT Forget.
make mom
Buy more Dino
Nugs. importent!

Diarrhe #6

is a relly good 1.
its during the hole
rise of my career so
their is lots of **adventure**
and **drama.** Tour drama,
Merch drama, Jerry
seinfeld drama, and
even chia Pet drama.
its from Like **2010-**
2015 or somthing. i
dont know exacly cuz
i dont Like math.

Dear Diarrhe,

i got the worst hatemail **EVER** today. it said im **NOT** Famus, it said im **ugLy**, and it said if i was any more inBred, i would Be a sandwich. i **DONT UNDERSTAND!** im pretty much the most Famus person in the world By now so i shouldnt Be getting Haters anymore! Even my mom said im Famus so it must Be true. Well, **GueSS WHAT?!** im gonna go on **MORE** tours, im gonna make **LOTS** of viral videos, im gonna sell **TONS** of merch, and im gonna Be more Famus then Beyonsay, oprah, and the taco Bell dog all comBined. **WATCH OUT HATERS! iM TAKING OVER THE WORLD & iM GONNA PROOVE YOU ALL WRONG!**

...Butt not today cuz i wanna Finish eating my pasghetti-o's.

♡ miranda

P.S. Not tomorrow either cuz i might Be tired.

123

Dear Diarrhe,

Sorry i havnt written in a while
Butt im a CELEBITY now so i have
a VERY BUSY SKEDULE! Uncle
jim says the next thing we need
to do for my career is make Brand
New, amazing, relly good merch. He
said shirts are overrated and dont
make good merch cuz not everyone
wears shirts. SO... whats the ONE
thing that EVERYONE has
in common?

The craving to Becum a magichan.
Thats rite! im gonna sell magic
kits, and im gonna make a FORTUNE!
a FOUND a magichan named Chris
Ballinger to help make the kits
Butt i decided not to pay him cuz
Being around me is payment pretty
much. its only fair. Also i want
all the money for myself.

Anyways, i taped all the tricks
from my magic kit to the next
page. OK By. ♡ Miranda

im so essited to Learn all these magic tricks!!!

MIRANDA SINGS MAGIC KIT

I HATE MAGIC!

Dear Diarrhe,

Magic is so DUMB! These tricks dont even work at ALL! im so titted off! i could do them FINE when we made the DVD with chris But Now none of the triks are working! THIS is a total Jip OFF! I've opend Like 20 magic kits and NONE OF THEM HAVE REAL MAGIC IN THEM! I'm so upset. i have been crying for a whole hour. And to top it all off, my mom took a sip of MY soda. she said "Oh! it was a acsident!" But Yeh Rite! This is a horibol day. i dont want to talk to you anymore Diarrhe, GOOD NITE! NOT Love, Miranda

actual Tears! im so upset!

127

♥♥ Dear Diarrhe, miranda Sings 2:111 pm

i Finally did it! i got a Famus BoyFrend! ~~my uncle~~ My Manager has Been trying to get me one For years Becuz it will help me to get more Famuser. Power couples are SO in right now. Soooo.... meet my new ♥BF♥ Joey ~~Graseffa, Grasefin, Grasefica Graserifina~~ Joey G. i met him a long time ago at one of his meet and greets Butt i got kicked out. Then i saw him at a taco Bell event and told him to collaB with me or ELSE! So he cummed over and we made this video.

iM SO ESSITED! WE ARE GUNNA GET MARRIED! ♡ miranda

P.S. Patrick is acting relly weird. just cuz HE was my BoyFrend First dosnt mean i can't have MORE Boyfrends. iM FAMUS! HeLLooo!? He cleary doesnt understand science.

⭐ **Dear Diarrhe,**

i have a **BOBBLEHEAD!** my Magic kits sold relly well, (like 20 or 21 kits sold so far) so my ~~uncle~~ manager thinks its time to add a new merch item. **BOBBLE HEADS OF ME!** He found a company in china that makes them 4 us. They are relly espensive 2 make, so to save money we are making mom package and ship them all from her Bedroom. ^{now} we wont have to pay someone to do all that. And hears the Best Part! Guess who was the First Person to Buy one? **LANCE BASS!** i think that means im offichally part of N'Sync!!!

♥ miranda

129

Dear Diarrhe,

im having a HORRIBOLE DAY! My uncle RUINED EVERYTHING! He Broke MY CHIA PET! He ran in to tell me something and nocked it off the shelf... and it spilled everyware and SHATTERD! He said it was a accident Butt i KNOW hes lying. Some of his clothes were on the floor so i kicked them relly hard as punishment. i just uploded a video telling my fans what happened. Here it is →

The comments are saying im Being overdramitic Butt im NOT! He ruined my Life and NOW i HAVE NOTHING TO LIVE FOR! sinserly, Miranda.

P.S. Patrick gave me that chia pet. ☺

Dear Diarrhe,

As you know, Life has Been hard for me recently. My chia Pet got ruined, my mom keeps annoying me, and i keep getting Hate mail! Hear is another 1 i got today.

anus 2 weeks ago
You remind me of me...
REPLY

i know that looks like a nice comment Butt dont Let it fool you. its from ANUS! i remind you of ANUS?! Thats not even the Best part of the Butt! RUDE!

Anyways, all this stuff has Been making me relly sad Lately. i cry about it alot and some times i feel like i should quit. (Dont you EVER tell ANYONE i said that. its a secret!) Butt i had a show at Birdland in NYC a couple days ago and my fans Brought me new chia pets cuz they saw my video about my Broken one. The haters are mean, my mom is annoying, Butt my fans make me feel like everything will Be ok.

They tell me i help them 2 Be confident and happy. They make me wanna keep going. They understand me, when no one else does. So ill never quit. i'll keep going for them, cuz they deserve it. Butt also cuz i want them to Buy me more stuff.

miranda

131

•..Dear Diarrhe,

i havnt written in a long time cuz i didnt want too. No offense. Butt a Lot has happened. i decided i shuld have a TV show aBout me. im talented, Pretty, and the most Famus person in the world so a TV show aBout me wuLd Be a HIT! So i started going to a Lot of different TV PLaces and told them to give me my own show and they said NO. What the heck! i dont no why every1 in this industry looks down on YouToBers. No one respects me! it makes no cents. i work so HARD every single day and still... No respect. its SO frustrating! im VERY TITTED OFF!

Love,
Miranda

P.S. i took this photo of myself today after i ate soup. →

Dear Diarrhe, Miranda S. i dont no the time.

i got a viral video Today!!! as you no, i love taking slurpee Baths. WELL, yesterday, decided to Film my slurpee Bath to Let my Fans no im a regular girl who takes Baths just like them! i guess everyone loved it cuz it got MILLIONS of views! People love QUALITY CONTENT!
Politicks? No thank you.
Talent? Boring!
Education? GOODBYE!
Taking a slurpee Bath with my clothes on? Millions of views! i think this is relly gonna help my career. Now ill definitly get the respect i deserve.

Love,
Miranda

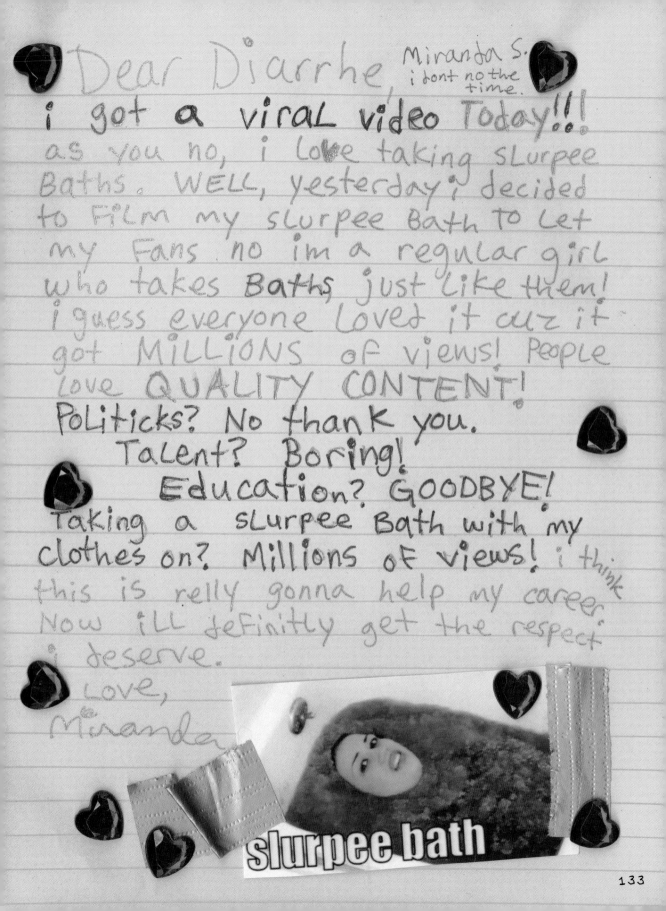

slurpee bath

133

Dear Diarrhe,

i decided to start touring alot more Becuz i love traveling and meeting all my Fans.

...Also i love money.

So im gonna start writing in hear aBout my Fun experiences on tour. Hear are some of the places im going in the next couple years—

♡ Miranda

CANADA

—seattle

—red deer

middle of nowear.

Toronto, eh?

—Portland

—Sacamento

Las vegas

—Salt Lakecity, UTAH

—BOLDER,CO

deBuqe, iowa

Madison, Wi

royal OKS, MI

Boston

Harrisburg

DUBLIN scotte

—Ptown

—NYC

iowa city

USA

kansas city

clevlend Ohio

washington DC

Albany pittsberg other

Europe

—sanafrisco

—Denver, CO

Nashville, TN

charlot NC

London

—LA

—Anaheim

—irvine

—san diego

—pheenix, AZ

Atlanta, GA

orlando

Norway

Austen, TX

Huston, TX

Fort lauderdale

HAWAii

Dear Diarrhe, ☺

Hi. Since im gonna start touring more i realized im gonna need ALOT of help. i have to hire someone to take care of travel details, get me water, fan me when im hot. etc, So i decided to get a Buttsistant. (i cant say the "A" word cuz its Bad and im not a sinner.) i Found a weird girl on YouTuBe and shes gonna cum on tour with me and Basicaly do everything i say. This is her

♡miranda applicachon

APPLICACHON TO WORK 4 MIRANDA

NAME: Rachel Ballinger

AGE: ~~22~~ No. You LOOK 23 →

FAVORITE COLOR: ~~Purple~~ Miranda

FAVORITE FOOD: ~~Pizza~~ Miranda

DO YOU LIKE ME: Sure. correct.

AS A FRIEND OR MORE: A Friend good

ARE YOU SUBSCRIBED TO ME?: Yes. good

WILL YOU DO EVERYTHING I SAY?: Sure.

HEADSHOT ←

your hair is too short. grow it out.

i dont like this shirt. Dont ware it again.

Your Hired.

Dear Diarrhe,

i Forgot to take this Diarrhe on tour, so i just wrote my diarrhe entrys on random things i could find on tour. i didnt journal every single day. just the days i could Find somthing to write on.

Dear Diarrhe, Miranda JuLy 12, 2012 11:02 Pm

i just FiNished my show in P-TOWN. when my uncLe told me i had a show there i got relly essited cuz a town all aBout Pee sounded relly Fun to Me. i ate a Lot of asparagus to prepare. Butt i got hear and was VERY disapointed. Their was NO pee. just Lots of haLF naked BOYS EVERY WHERE. i started to Freak out cuz i thot the P in P-towN stood For a Boy's privases. i started Praying For all the naked attraetive men imediatly and called my uncLe to Fire him Butt he said P-TOWN stands For

i Found this napkin in a drag Queens Bra

136

"PROVINCETOWN". He told me we only sold 16 tickets to my show and i needed to Beg in the streets Like a PEASENT! i Yelled in the streets For 6 hours! Naked men and Big Beautiful women with deep voices were everywhere. it was a intense day Butt sometimes you have to Sacrifise For your art. im still recovering Butt it was worth it.
After 6 hours OF misery Begging in the Streets, i sold 3 more tickets to my Show. Success.

♡ miranda

Dear Diarrhe,
Today i had a show in ATLANTA
Gorgia. it was a Christmas
show and i teched every1 the
REAL reason 4 the season...
giving me presents.

Something crazy happend
at my show. one of my
Fans got my autograph
tattood on his Leg!
Normally tattoos are a
sin But i think God
will Probly Let this
one slide.
♡ miranda

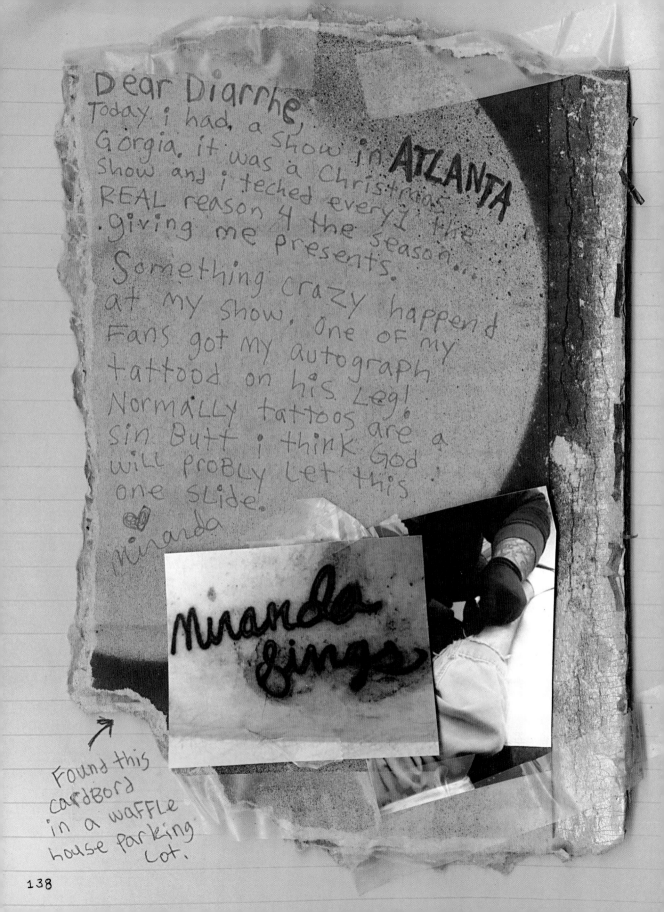

Found this
cardBord
in a waffle
house Parking
Lot.

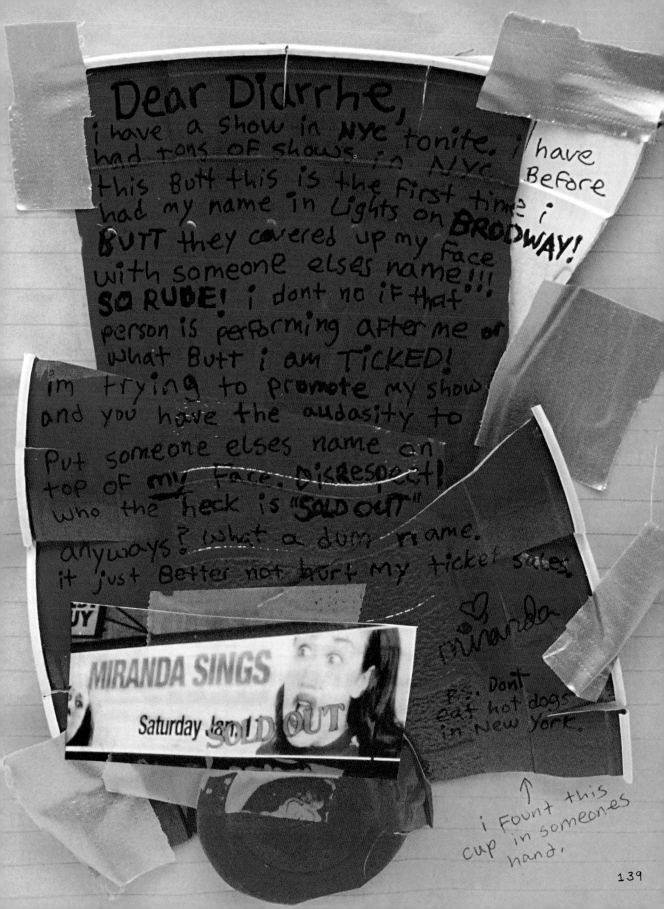

Dear Diarrhe,

i have a show in NYC tonite. i had tons of shows in NYC this Butt this is the First time i had my name in Lights on BRODWAY! BUTT they covered up my Face with someone elses name!!! SO RUDE! i dont no if that person is performing after me or what Butt i am TICKED! im trying to promote my show and you have the audasity to Put someone elses name on top of ~~my Face.~~ DISRESPECT! who the heck is "SOLD OUT" anyways? what a dum name. it just Better not hurt my ticket sales.

♡ miranda

P.S. Dont eat hot dogs in New York.

MIRANDA SINGS
Saturday Jan SOLD OUT

↑ i Fount this cup in someones hand.

Dear Diarrhe,
its Been a gr8 couple of days
i got to cum Back to London
Butt this time i came Back
with my Frend and BoyFrend
Frankie Grande.. We got
arrested at Customs cuz
the offiser thot i was
gonna Steal from the
country. just Becuz i said
a joke and said "im gonna
Steal all your money and not
pay taxes", doesnt mean its true.
he was So grumpy. Butt they
evenchally Let us go. My
Shows Sold out every NITE!
it was reLLY FUN.

I got this paper from dinner

140

and even though there is a huge language Barrier in London the audience still understood me relly goodly. My Fans are very smart. except when they dont give me presents. Then they R dum. ♥, Miranda

2 of my Fans. They r weird, But they Like me.

me and Frankie after we got aressted.

Dear Diarrhe,

i had a show in Detroit tonite and Rachel is SO GRUMPY. i thot we culd drive to all the shows this week cuz they are all in america. i got off stage, we got in the rental car, and i told Rachel to start driving. She said, "WHAT?! Thats 11 hours! Why are we driving and not FLYING?! Now i have to Drive thru the night and do a show TOMORROW with NO SLEEP?!" umm... get over it. She's such a BaBy.

How was i supossed to no the drive wuld Be that Far? anyways, im gonna go to sleep in the car now We have a Big day Zmorrow and i need my rest.

♡ miranda

HANDLES UP
NOT OUT

i found this Bag From a Lady with groseries.

Dear Diarrhe,

i performed in DuBuque, iowa today. The show was in a Movie theater. i performed iN Front of the screen where you watch Movies, and they didnt have spotLights so they just left all the Lights on in the hole theater. at First i was relly excited to Be in a movie theater cuz i thot i would get Lots of free popcorn. Butt i didnt. AND my dressing room was a projector room with nothing in it except a mattress with a Bunch of pee stains on it. and ONLY ONE of those stains was From me.

#TOURLiFe

♡ miranda

↑ i found this Box under the pee mattress

143

Dear Diarrhe,

We had a Emergency landing in Vegas yesterday on our way to Scotland because of tecknical difficulties. They said it was cuz a passenger's T.V. wasnt working butt i think it had to do with the fact that one of the wings was smoking. ANYWAYS, while we were waiting for our plane to get fixed, i found a nice spot on the ground by a trash can to eat my stale airport sandwitch. An angry lady in a beanie came up to me and told me i was destroying my tookie by sitting on the cement. She said there are chemicals in the cement that go up inside of girls and ruin there insides. She yelled at me for 15 minutes about it. Now, im no scientist, butt that sounds like a resipee to make a robot. i thanked her for the tip and sat there for 4 more hours hoping for the best.

Love,
Miranda

P.S. i didnt turn into a robot

← me licking the Edinburgh castle today.

144

❤ **Dear Diarrhe,** ❤

ive Been Touring <u>on</u> and <u>off</u> aLOT in the Last Few years and i <u>Love</u> it Butt im glad im home for a Little Bit. i decided to spend some time at home in tacoma to Focus on getting more Famuser and work on Becumming president. ALso i relly missed Patrick. i have <u>LOTS</u> of Boyfrends By now Butt he is my Favorite i think. (Dont tell him i said that.) He's the onLy one who makes me FeeL Like i have gas when im with him. its proBLy cuz he gives me Froze toes posickles and they have aLot of dairy in them. i took this picture for him 2day...→ i hope he Likes it.

Gotta go.. im Bored oF writing and my ❤ eye is ichy,

❤ ♡
miranda

145

Dear Diarrhe, Mirandasings Night time.

its Monday. That means i have 2 upload a video on my YouTube channel. UGH! why did i ever say i wuld do 2 videos a week? This is so much work and i am WAY TOO STRESSED to make a video today. My mom woke me up at 10:30 am when i was having a reLLy good dream. SO DisrespectfuLL! THEN there wasnt any "oops all Berries" Left so i had to eat plane "capten crunch". And After THAT i got a ich on the Bottom of my foot AFTER i put on my shoes. i wiggled my foot reLLy hard inside the shoe to try to get the ich Butt it didnt satisfy me at all. SO as you can see, im WAY too stressed to make a video... Butt I HAVE

146

too do it for my fans. im a slave to my work. How will my fans survive if i dont uplod a video??? They wont be able to function. ugh... im just gonna go film something relly fast and get it over with. BrB.

— — — — — — — — — — — —

ok, so i just quikly wrote a song and posted it. i did it in like 10 minutes and didnt relly care about it. Hopefully not too many people will see it. its called "Where my Baes at"

Gotta go...
mom made
Dino chicken
nuggets.
♡ miranda

p.s. my foot
still iches.

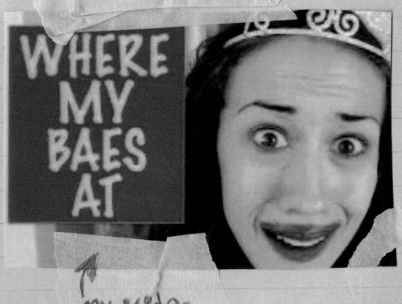

↑
my video

☺ Dear Diarrhe,

Miranda Sings
12:39 pm

Today somthing weird happend. A guy named jerry called me and asked me to get coffee with him. i never heard of him Before Butt someone told me he was a "comedien" so i thought i would try to help him get famus cuz i love charity work. We drove around in his weird little car for a while, got some coffee and he ate some gross diner food. i tried relly hard to help him with his career Butt i think he just doesnt have what it takes. Bless him for trying tho. Anyways, im starving so i gotta go. Bye.
♡ Miranda

P.S. i forgot what i was gonna say. Nevermind.

Dear Diarrhe,

my sister left this note on my Bed today. **SO** many things wrong with this! She went in to my room witch is **OFF LIMITS!**

> Miranda —
> I am so proud of you.
> Love you.
>
> ~Emily

she put something on my Bed and what iF i didnt see it? i could have choked on it in my sleep and **DIED!** or worse— i could have gotten a paper cut! she's **So rude!**

its relly weird how my Fans dont know about her... Butt she doesn't want anyone to know we are sisters cuz she's "emBarrased" of me.

This is hard for me 2 admit Butt... she's right. Being related to me **IS** emBarrassing. ☹

it must Be **so** emBarassing for her to Be related to someone who is way more talented, Pretty and perfect then her. poor girl...

i gotta admit— Life has Been crazy with all this Fame and its Been relly nice to know i have a sister around to annoy any time i want.

i relly dont Like her... Butt i **DO** Love her. (dont tell her i said that)

♡ miranda

149

☺ # Dear Diarrhe,

i was on the Jimmy Fallon show tonite. That old guy Jerry Seinfeld called me the other day and asked me iF i wanted to Be on the Jimmy Fallon show with him. i think MayBe the only way he wuld Be aBle to ~~the easiest~~ get on a Big show Like that is iF he had a Big CeleBrity with him. So naturaly he asked me. i played pictionary with Jimmy FaLLon, Martin short, and Jerry. on **LIVE TV!** i won the game i think. it was my First time on a talk show Butt i was the prettiest one their so they will proBly ask me to Be the New host soon. Jimmys cute and all... Butt im Better. No offense,

♡Miranda ☺

Dear Diarrhe,

its Been a while since i last wrote 2 you, Butt i have **Big News...**

NetFlix and HBO called. They Both want to do my T.V. show!

i dont no what to do. im so stressed. i have such a huge desicion to make. This could change my entire Life forever. should i have Mexican or italian Food for dinner? ugh...i cant decide.

Anyways, im gonna do the NetFlix Original series.

♡ miranda

151

Diarrhe #7

Fan male

Fan art

Miranda's Mirfandas!

Fan comments

Fan presents

This is my Fan Diarrhe

im relly Famus Now

so i have LOTS oF Fans

and they are always

giving me Letters,

art, presents, and a

Bag oF raw Bacon ona

i put a Bunch oF Fan

StuFF in this Diarrhe

to always remember

how Famus i am.

154

Dear Diarrhe,
i just got this Brand New
jurnal and i decided to
deadicate it 2 my Mirfandas.
in Case you dont no what
that is- hear is the definichon.

Mirfanda
(mer-fan-duh)
noun, verb, adjective, smart people and more

<u>Definichon:</u>
A person who is obsessed with the incredibel
superstar Miranda Sings. They love Miranda
more then anything in the world and they usually
dress just like Miranda and copy her because they
Are relly smart. d. Anyone who is not
a Mirfanda is a HATER and cannot be trusted.

MirFanda

155

its importent 2 no the diference Between a **FAN** and a **HATER**. You can tell By Looking at clues in the comments.

MiRFandas

They say nice things Like "OMG" (oh, Miranda's great)

They give you relly nice compliments.

Ricky Dillon ✓ · 3 years ago

omg

REPLY   722   👍 👎

Shanhanhania · 6 months ago
she looks like the type of girl who would microwave her pet hamster

REPLY   👍 👎

They say they Love you in every Language.

Adeleivalivas · 2 months ago
eres estúpido

They are vulnerabol and confide in you. i responded to Rylisom and told her to get a pad right away.

Rylisom · 3 days ago
When I here'd you sing my eras bled

REPLY   👍 👎

They say Bad words.

Kira 2 weeks ago
Miranda your stupid.
REPLY

They talk about gross things Like old people.

Wisemananan 2 weeks ago
I showed this to my grandma and she died laughing
REPLY

they Lie

Zoeeneeenee 9 hours ago
I hate u
REPLY

Jeanuijk 6 months ago
Y DO PEPOL WACH THIS STOOPID DUM BINCH
REPLY

They dont speak English good.

They dare you to do **very** offensive things.

XxBolBolaxX 2 months ago
I dare you to dab in one of your vids
REPLY 2

157

Fan Gifts

My MirFandas Love to give me Presents. Hear are some of My Favorites...

Lots of dolls of me

a nun

A sign 4 my Door

Fun handcuffs

ugly shirt from Jerry Seinfeild

Bag of hair

158

Drama Masks

Lots of hair clips

paper Mashay head with my real eyes inside

Lots of hand made clothes

MIRANDA
Lots of Braslets

a Little cake roll thats only a little smushed

A huge puppet of myself

a cat collar of someones dead Pet cat

Tiny crocks in case I ever shrink

159

Fan Letters

i get tons of letters from my fans every single day. They tell me how much they love me, they ask me 4 advice, tell me i save their lives and ask me to FOLLOW them on twitter. Here are some examples...

DEAR MIRANDA,
I AM YOUR #1 FAN! YOU ARE THE MOST TALENTED, BEAUTIFUL, PERFECT, AMAZING, INCREDIBEL, INSPIRING PERSON IN THE WHOLE WORLD AND I WILL NEVER STOP SUPPORTING YOU! LOVE YOU!
LOVE,
YOUR #1 FAN
UNCLE JIM

see? i save peoples lifes.

you shuld becum a orphan.

i lost this.

Dear Miranda,

Oh My gosh I cant believe I'm writing you a letter right now and you're actually reading it! You are my Hero. I am 14 years old and you literally saved my life. I'm dead ass serious you literally saved my life cuz like one day I was like really sad and Bad stuff and then I watched one of your videos and then I was like not sad and like you literally saved my life I'm not even kidding. My parents hate you and all my friends think you're lame so I'm not going to watch you're videos anymore. But I ... write and say ...s how my aunt died. It w... ou saved my honestly one of the worst days o... my life, but your videos made me ...f see why my smile when nothing else could. ...u. You're kind Thats why I want you to have ... and your lipstick my aunt's diamand necklace tha... ey and I dont was passed down to me. Please ...amous, but I'm take really good care of the ... you. Have a necklace. It means a lot to me. Also, since I gave you a real diamond can you ...ssa please follow me on twitters? and insta? and snapchat? If you dont, send me the necklace back. I don't want you to have it. Love you. ~Rachel

Follow me on twitter!

no.

Oh my gosh that must have Been so scary. i was Locked in the closet once for 2 hours and i was STARVING. Proud of myself for inspiring you to get out of the closet.

thank You!

Hi Miranda,

I just wanted to say thank you. Your confidence inspired me to come out of the closet. I finally feel free and happy. Living in fear and darkness for 15 years is finally over and I have you to thank for it. I l̶____ ____ the ____ of me ____ cult ____ First ____ at ____ as

Dear Miranda,

I am a stay at home mother of 3 young girls and I must say, I am extremely disappointed in the example you are setting for my children. I know you're very famous but that doesn't mean you can get away with this terrible behavior. My kids love your youtube show and watch it all day long while I'm busy. Yesterday I heard them watching a video where you were eating an unbelievable amount of candy. How dare you! My children are not allowed to have sugar and you put me in a very uncomfortable position where I had to explain to my 3, 5, and 7 year old that some people make the disgusting decision to put that poison into their bodies. THEN I heard you loudly singing a pop song. I do NOT let my children listen to pop music, but now they want to listen to it because of you. To top it all off, this morning I heard my 7 year old say "If someone like Miranda can be confident and become famous, I can do anything!". This is a horrible mindset to promote to children because it sets them up for failure. What if they want to be a youtube person or a pop star some day? That is an unrealistic goal and they will most likely end up with depression because of the false sense of hope YOU instilled in them. If my children grow up to be drug addicts, or in prison, I will be sending YOU the bill. You need to THINK about what you put on the internet for your millions of viewers. You are responsible for the lives of every single person watching you. GROW UP. If you had a yelp account I would give you ONE STAR!

Sincerely,
A very frustrated mother

These Kids sound relly smart. if this mom keeps Being a Butt ill take the kids. (Not relly i dont like kids. No offense)

162

Fan Art

i get thousands of fan
art drawings of myself
every year. Obviusly alot
of my fan art is on
the wall in my room.
Butt unfortunatly some
of my fans arent very
talented and they're
drawings arent worthy
of being on my famus
wall. i'll show
you what i mean...

ALICE · Age 2 · Dublin, irland

Jake·Age8·L.A.,CA

Rachel · 26 · Galt, CA

so you are LAZY. you didn't even color my skin peach color. I Look BLUE! your LAZY Rachel!

THANK you 4 giving me 3 privates. the extra ones under my knees look gr8!

why did you put hair under this arm pit but not the other one? LAZY! i shuld have hair under BOTH.

169

Parker • Age 4 • Santa Barbra, CA

Parker

Kory • Age 25 • Upland, CA

This drawling is relly good but you 4got to drawl my head and toes. i drew them 4 you. cut them out & tape them on the drawling. Take a PIC and TWeet it to me! @mirandaSings

#IFixedTheArt.

176

177

First of all, my forehead is MUCH bigger then this. You are lying to the world with this photo. FAKE NEWS!

I would Never wear grey eyeshadow so WHY did you drawl that? its UGLY

why didnt you put food in my mouth? You could have at least put a sausage in there or somthing. THINK Tyler. You want me to starve?

what am i Looking at? why do i look so scared? Why would you draw me looking scared? This drawing gets a F!

y do i have so many tiny eyebrows? its kinda cool but also I hate it.

Are these cockroches? raisens? Beans? chocolates? turds? What is in my hair?!?

This mouth is the only realistic thing on the entire face. My lips look very lutchus and my tong looks wet.

C+

Daisy • Age 12 • Sydney, Australia

182

FINALLY!
A good, perfeck, accurat drawling of me. This is exactly the size of my smart Brain so i love this drawling. Looks just lick me.

i lick how you made my eyelashes and eye brows blend together. cute.

183

184

so as you can see Diarrhe, some of my Fans have No Talent, some of my Fans have a little talent, and some of my Fans have lice... cuz i have it rite now and i hugged a lot of them at a show resently.

Butt even tho they can be annoying, i love my mirFandas. cuz without them, i wuld Be poor... and thats gross. No offence.
♡miranda

186

MirFandas = BFF

i gave them Lice.

i culd smell her meno-Pause.

he seems moldy.

she had wet skin

This photo gave me diaree-uh.

she made me itch.

she made me want 2 end the meet and greet.

i dont remember meeting her...

her Breth smelled Like old Bandaids.

she reminded me of a scaB

meeting him made me wanna eat hot dogs.

she smelled Like hamsters

Diarrhe #8 is
my current diarrhe, my First Bus Tour, Behind the scenes of my NetFlix show and my plans 4 the future are all in this Journal. its not finished yet cuz im still writing in it every Day Butt its relly good, no offense.

♥ Dear Diarrhe,

i got a Brand new Diarrhe! So ♥ much has happened. i wrote a BOOK! its called "Selp-Helf" its a BOOK on how to Be a human. ♥

i just Finished my Book tour at the mall of America and my Book PuBLishers just called. They told me ♥ im a New YorkTimes Best selling auther. i told them to change it to "Tacoma, Washington Times Best selling auther" Becuz im not from NYC Butt they Are dum and wont change it.
♥   idiots...
Love,
miranda

P.S. i dont no if you remember, Butt NetFLix is giving me my own show. We R Shooting it next year. it Better Be good or im Sueing.

Mood: good and hungry

Dear Diarrhe,

Guess what! i'm doing a BUS TOUR!
i've Been touring for years Butt
i have never done a Big Fancy tour
like this Before! i Feel like Aaron
Carter! One proBLem tho. They
said there is no pooping on the
Bus. Butt this tour is almost a
month long. These people must
have alien Butts cuz no one can clench
that hard for that long. i have
allready pooped twice and we
havent even Left the parking
Lot yet.

Anyways, i never got to do summer
camps when i was Little so i
decided to do my OWN summer
camp with my Fans For this
tour. Miranda CAMP!

♡ miranda

mood: excited
and constipated

192

i decided to have maching Frendship Braslets with all my Fans. We are selling these at all the shows.

This is a PP Patch my Fans can earn if they can earn if they partisipate... or if they Buy it.

MIRANDA SINGS PARTICIPATION PP PATCH SUMMER CAMP

These are the tour shirts. They have all my tour dates on the Back cuz i love gettin dat promo!

MIRANDA CAMP 2015

AUG 5 MINIAPOLIS, MN
AUG 6 GREEN BAE, WI
AUG 7 MILWALKEE, WI
AUG 8 CHKAGO, ILL
AUG 9 TOLEDO, O
AUG 11 CINCINATY, OH
AUG 12 COLUMUS, OH
AUG 13 REDDING, PA
AUG 14 NEW YERK CITY, NY
AUG 15 NORTHAMPTIN, MA
AUG 16 BOSTIN, MA
AUG 18 PHILIDILPHIA, PA
AUG 19 PHILIDILPHIA, PA
AUG 20 BELTIMORE, MD
AUG 21 RICHMUND, VA
AUG 22 NORFALK, VA
AUG 23 CHARLET, NC

This is what the stage looks Like! its Like actual summer camp Butt Better! cuz im at it.

MIRANDA CAMP!

195

Dear Diarrhe,

Bus tour is Fun, Butt im Freaking Tired! The dum Bus Driver keeps driving while im trying to sleep and its making my Bed move. So RUDE! We are over half way done with tour so i thot it wuld Be good to write down some of the memoraBel moments so Far —

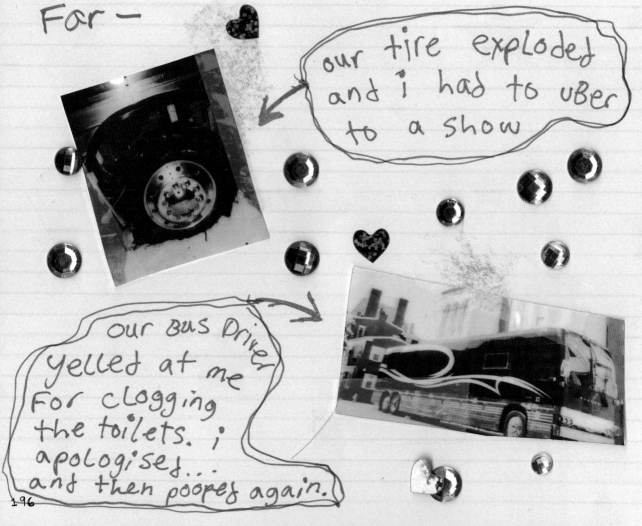

our tire exploded and i had to uBer to a show

our Bus Driver yelled at me For clogging the toilets. i apologised... and then pooped again.

196

we hired a Lady to give me a massage cuz ive Been VERY stressed and she just Poked my Forehead and heart for a hour and said, "you are healed" over and over. she smelled like mold.

Ben stiller came 2 my NYC show. i dont no who he is Butt every one was Freaking out. i think maybe this is him

This is what it Looks Like outside my BUS every Nite.

My Buttsistant told me she is quitting soon. So annoying. i dont no why anyone wuld want to quit working with me!

mood: Nothing

✪ Dear Diarrhe, miranda sings Aug 16, 2015 11:07.5PM

No offense, Butt this has Been one of the craziest nites of my Life. **i FAINTED ON STAGE!** well...tecknickly i wasNT on stage. i Left the stage in the middle of the show cuz i started feeling weird and i passed out rite when i got in the wings. Rachel had to go on stage and intertain the audience while i came Back to Life. i think i almost died proBLy. The doctor said i just had dehydration Butt i told him that wuld Be impossible cuz im a virgin. virgins dont get genitel diseases. its a Fact. Then he told me i need to drink more Liquids so this doesn't happen again, Butt i drink Like 7 sodas a day. AND tons of kool-aid. So

Basicly, he's a idiot. i was probly just poisened.

Anyways, After the show, i checked my phone and i had a text from Lilly Singh. it said, "Congrats! You won!" i thot she meant just winning at life so i was like "thanks." Butt then i found out i won A TEEN CHOICE AWARD! While i was Fainting i won the most prestigious award a celebrity can win. iCONiC. i cant wait to get my surfbord. i always wanted to add "surfing" to my list of talents. gotta go... this Bus is relly Bumpy and i need to poo again.

♡
Mirandde →

after i Fainted i got Back on stage AND Finishes the show

mood:
tired
happy
hungry
and

199

Dear Diarrhe,

i got home from Bus tour a couple months ago and got **RELLY BUSY** with the Netflix show. And since my dumB Buttsistant Rachel **QUIT** i had to hire a New Buttsistant. His name is **Kory** and he is relly cute. Hopefully he will get relly Famus so we can date some day. **(as you know, i only date famus people)** He's good at his joB Butt i relly miss Patrick Being my roadie. i fired him a long time ago cuz he cant help me with my quick changes Back stage untill we are married. **PLUS** he's allergic to milk.

♡ miranda

this is Kory.

mood: sticky

200

Dear Diarrhe,

OK, so remBer how Netflix told me they wanted to do a show aBout my Life? WELL i am TICKED OFF! i thot i wuld just make my own show and they wuld give me money to do whatever I want. Butt they hired a **cast**, a **crew**, and i have to move to VANCOOVER, Canada. They even gave us scripts! This is so annoying. OH! AND ANOTHER THING! They are telling a Bunch of secrets from my Life in this T.V. show! They want to show my S<u>ISTER</u>! Ugh. The only thing worse wuld Be if my Diarrhe's got Leaked. if that ever happened my Life wuld Be <u>over</u>! Anyways, i move to Vancoover to start shooting tomorrow. i'll tell you how it goes. i hope i understand the Language in Canada. ♡ Miranda

mood:
Ticked off and ichy

201

Dear Diarrhe,

we just Finished shooting the First episode. im SO TIRED! it took 4 days to shoot. That coleen girl is anoying Butt im glad she's hear cuz this is a lot of work and i dont wanna do most ~~scens.~~ scenes. (Dont tell her i said that.) ~~Anyways~~, hear are some pictures From set—

This is the cast. They r all kinda annoying Butt also nice.

They remade the Fish store my uncle worked at. exsept its Fansier and has more Living Fish.

This is the set of my room. i hate it cuz it dosnt have a roof. just Lights.

♡ miranda

mood: exausted

202

● Dear Diarrhe,

im so Freaking annoyed! Filming this show is dum! i will do a scene and the directer will say "Cut!" and then make us do it again and again and again! i allready did it once! why do i have to do it a million times? Especially if i lived it For REAL? so glad its almost over. Butt im essited to have my own Netflix original series.
    Miranda is the new BLACK.

Filming episode 2. They got mad cuz i kept singing after they yelled "cut". Butt they shuld have been THANKING ME! i gave them a free consert!

me and Patrick. He Looks esactly Like him. 😊

♡ miranda

mood: relly ~~happy~~ annoyed

203

Dear Diarrhe,

Tonite was the premeer of the NetFlix show. That dum Collen girl showed up Looking Like a total skank. i could see her entire chestickles. She Looked Like a skin colored sausege Link. → She's so anoying! We had a deal and she keeps trying to cum in and steal my thunder, and take all the credit. She's relly Confusing my Fans! some of them think shes Me! ugh. Anyways the Show is relly good (oBviusLy) and i Love my Fans so MUCH! without them it never wuld have happened. Also they give me presents. Gotta go. Mom made a canned Food Buffet to celebrate. ♡ miranda

mood: happy

Dear Diarrhe,

im in the land **of SiN** doing a show yup. **Vegas.** ive Been praying relly hard for all the sinners hear Butt decided to take a Break to Let you no that **NetFLiX called** and we are getting a seasoN 2 of Haters Back oFF! That means i am offishally the First YouTuBer in <u>History</u> to get her own TV show picked up for a second season on NetFliX Called Haters Back off starring Miranda Sings! Butt i relly hope they dont put me in the Guinness Book of world records cuz i do <u>NOT</u> Like Beer. ♡miranda

P.S. My show in vegas went relly good even tho it was FuLL of sinners.

mood: sweaty

205

Dear Diarrhe,

WELP, im on set for **Season 2** of Haters Back OFF, and once again, the crew is making this WAY more harder then it needs to Be. This is why i wanted to do everything MYSELF! OK hears a example—

~~#####~~ We are doing a episode aBout when i wore a taco costume and had a protest.

SO FIRST— the writers drew the Logo of the taco resterant.

THEN—they drew the costume on the Back of the script and sent it to the costumer. it Literly looks nothing Like me.

NEXT—they made a tiny doll version of the costume

FINALLY— i got to ware the costume Like a month Later

See? So over-compicated. i toLd them to just make it out of paper or just do CGI Butt no one Listened to me. Literaly EVERYTHING in the show is Like this. So **COMPLiCated!** ugh.

mood: every1 is dumB.

♡ miranda

206

Dear Diarrhe

i just realized i never even told you about all the collabs i Been doing since i Been getting more Famuser. i Have TONS of new Baes, and some new emenies. Hear are some of the peopol i have collaBed with.

jojo: emeny

gaBBie: emeny

maddie zeegler: Frend kinda

James Charles: sister

scott and mitch: Baes

Lilly sing: Bae

ricky dillon: Bae

Grace Helbig: i dont no

rosanna pansino: chef

Hannah hart: drunk emeny

GloZell: BFF

Joeys pooping dog: Bae

Theres alot more Butt i forgot. Anyways, i got 2 announce the date my NetFlix show season 2 preemeers. it was on a popsickle stick. i Live streemed me eating it... Afterwords i sat alone for 6 hours. sometimes Being me is Lonely. Butt then i realized your never alone if you have food. so i ate more popsickles

♡ miranda

MOOD: Gassy.

octobur 20

Dear Diarrhe,

Season 2 came out and im incredibol in it, no offense, Butt they DELETED SCENES! There was a scene where i was dancing and singing with all these sexy Boys and it got CUT! Probly cuz i was just too good and it made every1 else Look Bad.➤

and they also cut a scene where we threw a Birthday party For my mom, and that got cut too!➤

at Least i have some secret rehersal Footage of ~~Coalen~~ ~~Collen~~ that dum girl doing the dance numBer... i wish i had Footage of me doing it cuz im WAY Better. 🌸
mood: amazing

♡ miranda

Dear Diarrhe,

i havent written to you in a while Butt
dont worry, not much has happened...

- i interviewed celebrities on the red carpet
  for **ELLEN**
- i went on the **Jimmy Fallon** show 2 times.
- i was on "**Live with Kelly and Ryan**"
- i hit **8 Million** subscribers on YouTube
- i have **6.5 million** insta followers, and **2.7 million**
  ~~million followers~~ twitter followers.
- i didnt get a season 3 of **Haters Back off.**
- i pretended like i didnt care Butt i cried alot.
- i went on a **sold out world tour.**
- i found a **flea** on my cat.
- i got a lot more famus **Boy frends**
- got nominated for a Bunch of awards.
- i got a hangnail on my pinky toe wich i
  didnt even know was possiBol.

See? Not much happened, Butt this pinky
toe hangnail situation is relly
upsetting me. i tried ripping it out
Butt it star**t**ed to Bleed. **ugh...** Jesus
Take the Wheel! **why does Bad stuff
always happen to good people?!?**
please pray 4 me.

♡ miranda

mood: Bloody.

209

WeLL Diarrhe,

i've Been doing alot of thinking lately and its exhausting. Butt also i realized something. When i First started out on YouTuBe no one respected YouTuBers. NoOne would take us seriusly. Butt the whole internet comunity knew that if we just worked hard, stayed Patient, and Found success, one day... we wuld Be respected. One day... we wuld Be taken seriusly. One DaY... we wuld get the recognition we deserve. Well Diarrhe, i've Been on YouTuBe For 10-ish years and the ~~day~~ day is Finally here... where i realize its never gonna happen. its 2018 and the onLy YouTuBers in the news are rich young white Boys doing relly Bad immature stuff. They are making the rest oF us Look Bad... And it is HARD to make me Look Bad. ↘

Now im No scientist Butt Last time i checked, i wasnt a rich, young, immature white Boy so i gotta Figure out a way to stay **Famus!** Now i oBviusly conkered **YouTUBe**, NetFLix, world Tours, merch, reLationships, and writing a Book, so its time for me to get creative and plan out the next Big thing in my career. So hear are some of my **TOP SECRET** ideas to Becum a Famus iconic Legend.

Viral video ideas

⭐ - stare at camera without BLinking for 30 minutes challenge

⭐ - Try Fitting whole Foot in mouth challenge.

⭐ - eat Lunch

Tours

⭐ i allready Been to Europe, Austrailia, New zeeLand, america, and canada. im pretty sure thats the hole earth. So my Next tour... wiLL Be in **SPACE!**

MOVIES

⭐ i dont no how this is possible Butt i still havent made a movie. it has to Be BIG so i need to think outside the Box and Be original. SOOO... hears what im thinking. Everyone makes movies with awake people. so im gonna do a whole movie of me sleeping! it will Be iconic cuz no one has done it Before #genious

iNVenchoNs

⭐This is the most exciting thing of all. im gonna start inventing stuff so i can add **inventer** to my talent List. Hear are some of my genious invenchons so Far...

⭐THE SLEEP IN ALARM⭐

what does everyone want? MORE SLEEP! so i want to invent a aLarm that goes off 2 hours after the time you set for it to go OFF. That way you get 2 more hours of sleep Butt no one can get mad at you if your late to stuff cuz it was the aLarms FauLt. #geniousinvenchom

212

⭐BATH BOMB DINNER⭐

Everyone Loves Bath Bombs and everyone Loves eating, so i want to combine the two. Bath Bombs usually just squirt out a color, Butt how cool would it Be if they squirted out a taco?! or a Burrito? or Lasania? You could take a Bath and go under water with your mouth open and get a mouthfull of ground Beef. im gonna make a ~~FORCHUNE!~~ FORTUNE!

⭐EDIBLE MOLD⭐

im sick of throwing away perfectly good food just Becuz mom said it got some mold on it. So i want to invent edible mold! Your food will never go Bad again! it will just get delishiously Fuzzy.

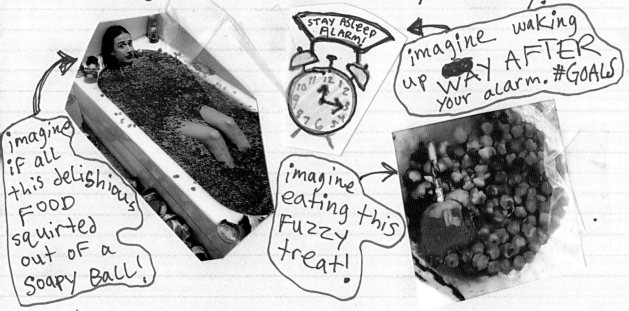

imagine if all this delishious FOOD squirted out of a soapy Ball!

STAY ASLEEP ALARM!

imagine waking up WAY AFTER your alarm. #GOALS

imagine eating this Fuzzy treat!

So Di'arrhe, as you can see, i have some pretty amazing plans and my career is about to **EXPLODE!** Oh! And guess what else? i dont have Haters anymore! i realized the people saying mean and rude things about me arent Haters at all! They are actually **SUPER FANS!** Think about it. They wach all my videos, they always comment, they always tweet me, they know everything about me, and they are totally obsessed with me. **THATS A FAN!** So to all those haters who keep saying "give up!" or "get off YouTube" or "go away No one Likes you", **DONT WORRY.** i will never stop working hard and Being Famus cuz i no <u>YOU</u> would miss me the most.

Gotta go. mom made tator tots for dinner and i have a SCAB to pick.

mranda

P.S. im perfect.

mood:
unstopable
happy
grateful
hopfull
gassy